The Visceral Experience

A Philosophy of Energy and Reality

The Visceral Experience

A Philosophy of Energy and Reality

BY
DANIEL D. BARBER

Hand Drawn Illustrations by
Angela M. Barber

Graphics by
Daniel D. Barber

Cover Image Courtesy of ESA/Hubble

Visceral Experience Press

ISBN: 978-0-692-30676-5

With Love To Ann, Anja and Elena

Table of Contents

Daniel D. Barber

Acknowledgments

There is no way that I could have gained knowledge of The Visceral Experience without numerous teachers that I have encountered throughout my life, or support from my family and friends. Although some of the lessons were hard earned or slow to sink in (in fact, I struggle daily to overcome my natural predisposition) I have made progress. I would like to thank, first and foremost, my wife, Angela, for her support throughout our marriage and especially while I took time away to write this book. She provides a daily example on being a kind, loving, patient and forgiving being. I'd like to thank my children for daily lessons in love, spontaneity and joy. They have taught me more about patience and love than I ever thought I would know. I would like to thank my in-laws for the unending support they have shown their daughter and me over the years. I couldn't have married into a better family. They have been an unflagging source of light in my children's lives. I would also like to thank all of the people who took part in my growth in energy work over the years — knowingly or unknowingly.

iv

The Visceral Experience

The energy of the mind is the

essence of life.

~Aristotle

Daniel D. Barber

The Eye of Infinity

As a man who has devoted his whole life to the most clear headed science, to the study of matter, I can tell you as a result of my research about atoms this much: There is no matter as such. All matter originates and exists only by virtue of a force which brings the particle of an atom to vibration and holds this most minute solar system of the atom together. We must assume behind this force the existence of a conscious and intelligent mind. This mind is the matrix of all matter. ~Max Planck

I had just fallen asleep, or so it seemed, when I was awakened by a powerful surge of energy through my body. I experienced it as an inch-thick shaft of orange energy surging up through my spine from my tail-bone to the crown of my skull. It exploded as a brilliant, blinding light in my brain and then... darkness — nothingness. I was no longer in my body, or in my bedroom even. I was in a never-never world of darkness; incorporeal, though I felt as solid and as in control of my senses as I do right now while writing this. I felt the weight of gravity as I stood absorbing the event and though I was surrounded by infinite darkness I was not in the dark myself. I was on an island in the void, waiting. Only moments had passed when, from behind me, I felt a hand come to rest on my right shoulder and a

2

powerful male voice, comforting in timbre, asked, "Should I accept you into my heart?" After a moment of careful consideration (For reasons I'll explain shortly I actually weighed outcomes in my mind before settling on an answer), I answered, "Yes." With my answer, I was hit by a tremendous explosion of energy at my crown and third eye. This time when my senses cleared I could only observe passively as I was enveloped by what I call the 'Eye of Infinity'.

It was a staggeringly beautiful geometric design of light and dark which fairly *pulsated* with power. As beautiful as it was, the design lacked any sense of symmetry that I could discern. On the top and left of a circular white field were two large rectangles perpendicular to each other. The rest of the white field was covered by smaller geometric shapes. The large rectangular designs are what impacted me the most and I remember them clearly. The specifics of the smaller designs were perhaps too much for my consciousness to retain. The lines were glowing with a bright maroon light as if there was an incandescent force behind the design pushing the shapes out. In that infinite instant in which it approached and finally overtook me I became a part of it and it became a part of me. I woke shortly after with energy still buzzing through my body. With the intensity of the experience and with the surging flow of energy, sleep did not come quickly that night.

Unfortunately, words are simply too shallow to describe the experience adequately. On the facing page is my best effort at reproducing the design in two dimensions:

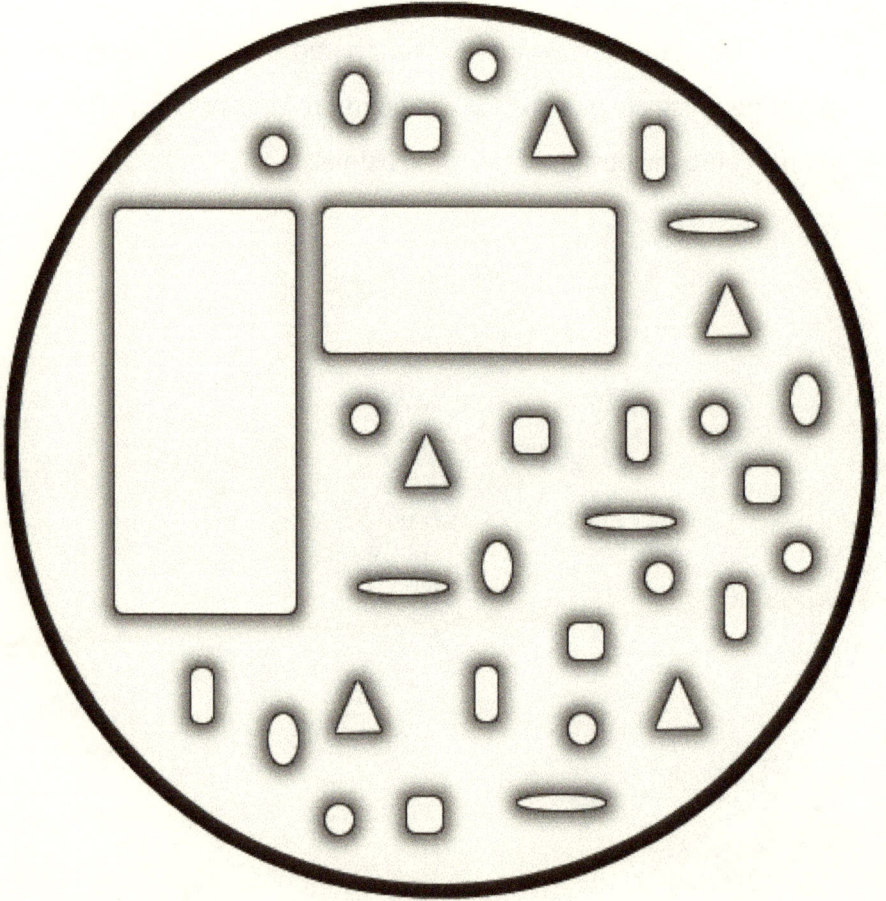

Eye of Infinity

As I reflect back on this experience several thoughts rise to mind.

The striking similarities that this experience exhibits with many different realms of human spiritual belief identifies it as a primal experience, perhaps one of many, from which many spiritual, religious, and philosophical traditions arise. Carl Jung might have called it an archetype. It is a nearly typical 'Kundalini Awakening' as described by many eastern mystics. Were I a Christian or a Muslim it would be labeled a divine vision. If it had followed the ingestion of the brew ayahuasca used by amazonian shamans it would be considered a visit with the Mother. And if it had followed the inhalation of Dimethyltryptamine (DMT) smoke it would be considered by psychonauts (explorers of hallucinogenic drugs) to be a 'breakthrough' experience.

There is no question that I was in an alternate reality as I stood there in the darkness. The feeling is not something that is even closely approximated by the dream state, lucid dreams, or even by an out-of-body experience (OBE). I have never before paused to consider the ramifications of my actions when in a dream (for me, and I suspect for most others, the dream state is typically amoral). While OBE I have never had another entity approach and interact with me, and I have never *not* been in control of events. With the exception of having answered the question as I chose, I was fully at the whim of this foreign entity.

The structure of the question posed by the entity is striking to me — in that it is the opposite of the standard Christian dogma of "Will you accept Jesus into your heart?" If the entity with whom I interacted was Jesus then it was he who *accepted me* into his heart, not the other way around. Does tradition somehow get this wrong? Is the form of the question dependent upon the person or some other factor of which I am unaware? I have not mistaken the question, as it was this reversal that caused me to pause before answering. It is an intriguing possibility that an early Christian misremembered after having experienced a similar event.

The special place that geometric patterns hold within the Muslim religion is also worthy of remark. The prohibition against the use of likenesses is not addressed in the Quoran, but was introduced in a later tradition (called *hadith* in the arabic). The use of geometric patterns were adapted instead. Is it possible that this particular hadith was added by a believer with an experience similar to mine?

It was only after having my vision that I discovered that users of the drug Dimethyltryptamine (DMT) have reported similar, if not the very same, sequence of events (though not the same geometric pattern) during their 'breakthrough experiences' (an experience in which one 'breaks through' indicates the user entered an altered state of consciousness). A hypotheses has been proffered that DMT is a substance organic to the human body produced by the pineal gland under certain, perhaps extraordinary, conditions. My experience, and that of others who report visions, might be proof that DMT is organically and naturally produced. It has also been hypothesized that DMT is always being produced at just the right amount within our brain to produce our everyday consciousness, an irony that is worthy of remark: should this be the case, then our everyday physical reality is the direct result of a hallucinogenic drug!

While relatively new to western science, the relationship between DMT and consciousness has been exploited by amazonian shamans for thousands of years in the form of ayahuasca. Ayahuasca is a brew made of various native plants that contains both DMT and a natural monoamine oxidase inhibitor (MAOI) which allows the hallucinogen to be effective when ingested orally, and the experience therefore to last hours longer. Shamans in other parts of the world use the hallucinogens that are readily available in their locale. For example American Indians use peyote, and shamans from Oaxaca, Mexico utilize salvia divinorum.

Objectively, of all the religious and spiritual traditions, my experience conforms most closely to the 'Kundalini Awakening' as described by Indian mystics in the Hindu religious texts The Upanishads. My awakening, thankfully, was fairly gentle when compared to some of the horror stories told by those who have had theirs spontaneously thrust upon them. Awakenings are generally considered to be accompanied by psychic powers, everlasting joy, and communication with spiritual entities. I can tell you that mine was accompanied by personal growth, the resolution of some of my most severe childhood traumas, the departure of significant anger, and, yes, even an increase in psychic ability.

The vision however was atypical of an awakening. I tend to think of it in terms of a software patch that was loaded when I hit a certain milestone in my life or energetic ability. It did not come with any clear communication or instructions. I do feel that since then something inside me changed or improved — that I have been observed and found to be worthy (although worthy of what I don't know). And I hope to experience something similar again in the future. And maybe, just maybe, one day I'll be able to look back and discern the meaning — to mark the change that occurred. It is the prospect that this event was the harbinger of profound change that will keep me pursuing energy work and healing. Perhaps my next experience will come with a clearer message.

How is it that I have come to achieve my Kundalini Awakening at the fairly youthful age of forty-three with no background in Hinduism or other Eastern Indian spiritual teachings? I am nothing special — no more special than any of you reading this book. I have not dedicated my life to any theology nor do I have a special pedigree wherein power has been handed down from my forefathers. I don't dress differently (unless you consider jeans and t-shirt to be different) and I don't pray, tithe, or sacrifice animals. I am the same as you. I was able to achieve these results by using the process I lay out in the pages ahead. What follows is a framework for achieving spiritual growth that is not encumbered by unnecessary ceremony or the need to learn esoteric terms.

You, Quantum Computer

Daniel D. Barber

The User Manual

Even sleepers are workers and collaborators in what goes on in
the Universe. ~Heraclitus

We have in our possession one of the most sophisticated quantum computers in existence. It is self-replicating, self-cleaning, self-regulating, constantly regenerating and capable of reproducing near exact copies of itself. Indeed, many times our 'copies' feature attribute improvements and refinements not available in the previous model. I certainly know that this is true of mine.

Each of the atoms in each of our cells, regardless of cell type, interfaces directly with The Quantum. The atoms of our cells interpret our will and intent, distill them into commands and then pass those commands into The Quantum. The Quantum accepts these commands and executes them. Sometimes the commands are strong, powerful, well-defined and beneficial — and sometimes they are not. The Quantum doesn't care either way. Like a computer it will do exactly what it is instructed — nothing more and nothing less. And like a computer it will execute even commands that are harmful to the user. The Quantum is indifferent to the reality it creates.

The only real difficulty in running your quantum computer (much of which is done automatically for you) is in learning how to properly design and format the commands that should be passed to The Quantum. Mankind's struggle is *not* the lack of a powerful enough computer; our struggle is one of not having a *user manual* for this infinitely powerful machine that each of us does possess.

The ideas and processes in this book are an effort, like many books that have gone before, to create that manual for your quantum computer. It is my hope the framework that follows will add appreciably to the current state of knowledge dedicated to correctly interfacing with The Quantum.

Daniel D. Barber

In short, the framework of **The Visceral Experience** is as follows:

> Uninhibited energy flow + (advanced visualization and powerful intention) **results in** a viscerally experienced reality (an intense gut feeling).
>
> This viscerally experienced reality **results in** dissonance with current reality.
>
> This dissonance **results in** a merging of current reality with viscerally experienced reality.
>
> This merging **results in** a new reality.

By consciously creating a strong somatic effect (gut feeling) within ourselves which mirrors the gut feeling we would have if our desired intentions, expectations and feelings were already extant we have a method for managing, or even manipulating, our reality. This somatic effect is our interface into The Quantum. This is how we pass commands, for good or ill, to the universe.

14

The technology of The Visceral Experience is the most effective method for creating the necessary *strong* somatic effect in order to consciously manifest your desired reality.

Evolution

There are some people who live in a dream world, and there are some who face reality; and then there are those who turn one into the other. ~Desiderius Erasmus

Welcome to the next step in your evolution as a human being. What I am about to present is a technology for interacting with and managing your personal reality. The Visceral Experience represents a paradigm shift in our understanding of the world and reality, and a significant transformation in our relationship with the world and each other.

On the macro-cosmic level The Visceral Experience is a transformation of mindset from "I am separate" to "We are one"; it is experiential proof that we are all one energy and that we are all part of the infinite.

On the microcosmic level The Visceral Experience is a metamorphosis from "I can't do it," or "I'm not seeing the promised results," to "Whoa, this works!" and "That's crazy! I can do that!?" It is the foundation for successful realization of numerous, if not all, psychic related pursuits, from manifestation to out-of-body experience to remote viewing. And it is the basis for the significant spiritual growth which will accompany your progress every step of the way.

Beyond that, the ideas in this book will allow you to redefine in a more positive manner how you perceive life and reality. We have all heard the saying "Perception is reality". I would submit that *The Visceral Experience **is** perception **is** reality*. I am not just guessing here; I'm speaking from experience.

The knowledge that follows in this book has been gleaned from over twenty years of working with different skill sets in anything and everything that has to do with naturally expanding the mind. The Visceral Experience is a combination of different techniques that, when used in conjunction with each other, put an order of magnitude more power at your fingertips. This technology is visualization on steroids or nuclear powered manifestation.

Some of the skills you will have heard of, and will have probably practiced before, like affirmations, setting intentions and basic visualization. Others, like perceptual positioning and sensory sub-modalities, might be new to you. I have spent much time gathering and sharpening the best techniques of those available in order to present you with the most effective methods. These techniques are included as exercises in each section so that you can begin using them right away.

I have combined them into a framework that can be used at will to create or alter your personal reality. I will caution you, though, that this is not magic. It is a technology that must be learned and practiced for there to be any appreciable results.

It is also the purpose of this book to dispense with obfuscating ceremony and needless esoteric terms. Though I do use terms like *chakra, subtle energy body* and *enlightenment they* are either well known or serve their purpose well.

If you have the time and resources, find copies of the books I mention in the following text and read them for yourself. While I will delve into the individual methods as much as I can it is inescapable that I will miss something the original author would never leave out. I certainly do not intend to go into the same detail those authors did in describing their methods. Additionally you may realize or come to understand a facet of a particular method which I have missed. In any case a more thorough understanding of each method can only benefit you as you grow in your ability and experience.

Go to these source materials and pull from them what you can — what is important to you in your path. You may discover a completely new and different application that is entirely your own.

Please keep in mind that as much as this book talks about psychic experiences and capabilities, it is far more about spiritual growth and the path to enlightenment. As you learn the methods of **The Visceral Experience** and grow in the skills necessary to achieve psychic results you will be challenged to better yourself and to confront traumas experienced throughout your life. These past traumas will rise unbidden, one after the other, as you progress through this process. If you are able to move past one trauma another will rise in its place. This is a natural process which everyone must go through to experience growth.

The Visceral Experience

What we achieve inwardly will change outer reality. ~Plutarch

Shortly after graduating from high school nearly thirty years ago, I joined a skydiving club. All in all I jumped seven times, but it is the sixth time that sticks in my memory so many years later. After five static-line jumps, where the cord is pulled automatically as you exit the aircraft, this sixth jump was my first free fall; I had to pull the cord myself.

On this first jump into nothing I was so completely focused on pulling the cord that, when I reached for it, I broke my arch (the arch of your back when skydiving determines your center of gravity and whether you fall looking down or looking up) and consequently flipped over such that I was falling face-up. As I completed the maneuver, and actually pulled the cord, the parachute deployed, but instead of coming over my shoulders it came out under my feet. This caused me to flip in my harness (think suspenders here) thereby reversing my risers, which is how the direction of flight is controlled. Fortunately, after I overcame my shock of being flipped upside down, I was quickly able to figure out how to control my flight. I landed safely. Besides being a little shaken it was not a big deal. I quickly moved on to my seventh jump which went off without a hitch.

Years later while recounting this story for a friend of mine I found my heart began to beat very rapidly, I broke out in a cold sweat and I even experienced a quick bout of dizziness. In effect, as I was telling this story to my friend, I was also somatic-ally re-experiencing the event. For me this was my first *significant* experience with the so-called mind-body connection. What I didn't know at the time was that this connection is bi-directional; somatic experiences can also affect reality.

A decade later and newly out of the army I decided that I needed to do something to stay in shape. I was burned out on running and lifting weights and wanted to try something different. Yoga intrigued me as some of the people I knew who did yoga seemed like they were in much better shape than I had ever been even at the height of my physical conditioning. After a quick search I was able to find a Yoga teacher of some thirty years experience just down the road from me. He taught a style called Kundalini yoga which focuses heavily on breathing and moving 'energy'. I didn't really know what was meant by 'energy', but regardless, I was soon signed up and attending his classes.

It was not long, maybe a month or two, before I first started to experience lucid dreaming. Lucid dreaming is the experience of being aware in a dream to the point that you realize you are dreaming and can then control the events of that dream. In one lucid dream I still recall clearly after so many years, I remember causing, on purpose and purely by thought, an elevator to appear in a building wall because I did not want to climb the stairs. Lucid dreaming was fun and exciting, but not particularly paranormal in my opinion. I would look forward to going to bed every night on the possibility of experiencing a lucid dream. Being single at the time, I had no other reason to particularly look forward to going to bed!

Lucid dreaming opened my eyes to something new and I began to research and read everything I could about all types of altered reality experiences — anything at all I could find that related to, or expanded upon, the concept of lucid dreaming. This is when I discovered what is commonly called the out-of-body experience (OBE). Soon, I had purchased a copy of the book *Adventures Beyond The Body* by William Buhlman and after reading and practicing his methods for no more than a couple of weeks I had my first OBE.

Daniel D. Barber

The first time I went out-of-body the experience hit me like a ton of bricks; OBEs drastically affected my understanding of reality. I quickly expanded my exploration beyond my former boundaries for explanations of how reality worked. I became preoccupied with reading about and investigating lucid dreaming and OBEs which had the further effect of increasing their frequency. Using the methods William Buhlman discusses in his book, I was able to gain a scintilla of control during my experiences. It was this ability to control my environment while OBE that convinced me that what I was experiencing was significantly different from and more powerful than a dream state.

All in all it only took three weeks from the time I first set my intent until I experienced my first OBE. I discuss this more in Powerful Intent.

Unfortunately I soon began a new job that dominated my attention for the better part of a year and my exploration into matters of the mind took a back seat to more mundane concerns. It took me nearly five years to re-focus and delve back into these wonderful and amazing experiences.

Around the same time I was reading books written for the lay person on quantum physics and neuro-linguistic programming (NLP). Completely separate fields of study, right? Not so. A basic understanding of each of these fields has contributed to my ability to make a stronger use of the human energy field and eventually led me to formulate what I call **The Visceral Experience**.

So what is The Visceral Experience? Simply put, it is a combination of the disciplined exercise of **advanced visualization** techniques and the willful and powerful anchoring of desire into **intention**, both working on a foundation of the **uninhibited flow of energy** innate within us all. The exercise of these two skills, in combination with unrestricted energetic ability, creates an intense and realistic gut feeling — a gut feeling that mirrors the gut feeling you would have if your desired reality was, in fact, your current reality. It is this gut feeling which causes change to happen and The Quantum to act. A successful use of The Visceral Experience fools the mind into believing that whatever you are imagining *is* reality, which in turn, compels the "current reality" to adjust to this "new reality" in order to remove the discrepancy.

Daniel D. Barber

The Visceral Experience:

Uninhibited energy flow + (advanced visualization and powerful intention) **results in** a viscerally experienced reality (an intense gut feeling).

This viscerally experienced reality **results in** dissonance with current reality.

This dissonance **results in** a merging of current reality with viscerally experienced reality.

This merging **results in** a new reality.

… is comprised of the following flow (skills to results):

Maintained Relaxation

Plus

Light Trance

Plus

Self Energy Work

begets

Uninhibited Energy Flow

Uninhibited Energy Flow

Plus

The combination of Advanced Visualization and Powerful

Intention

begets

The Visceral Experience

The Visceral Experience

equals

Reality

Daniel D. Barber

Relaxation

Without the ability to reach a state of sustained relaxation you have no foundation from which to work. The moment you lose a relaxed state of being is the moment you are grounded back in your current reality. Even advanced psychic practitioners need to be in a relaxed place in order to practice successfully. They are able to relax their physical body almost immediately upon starting such that their meditation and energy work can proceed quickly, undisturbed by physical or mental discomfort.

The enemies of relaxation are various ranging from muscle cramps to everyday concerns and worries. Yoga is the answer at which ancient practitioners of meditation arrived. They surmised that the more physically fit you are, the less you will be distracted by physical irritations. This is also the genesis for the yogic insistence that eating super healthy will make one enlightened. It won't. It will simply allow one to meditate longer without uncomfortable bellyaches — unless you count the bellyache of an empty stomach. Unfortunately for many, yoga has come to be seen as the end goal rather than as a stepping stone toward a deeper benefit.

That's not to say that exercise and healthy eating do not have an effect on spiritual growth. I believe they do, but I do not believe they are prerequisites. You do not need to be a vegan yoga guru in order to progress spiritually. What I have found is that, as you progress spiritually, you naturally become predisposed towards exercise and eating healthier. Does it hurt to start early? Not at all, but don't count on it as a leg up.

> The goal of maintained relaxation, in regard to The Visceral Experience, is to be able to achieve a state of relaxation quickly and to maintain that state regardless of what is going on with your physical, mental or energetic bodies.

Trance

Clearing the mind and achieving a restful and relaxed trance state is an integral part of every psychic-related skill of which I am aware. When our minds are chaotic with everyday thoughts and concerns our ability to separate ourselves from our ego is limited. The separation from ego — the metamorphoses from actor to observer — is critical for allowing the expansion of your perception of both internal and external states.

One of the nice things about meditation is that, once you have internalized the method, it can be 'anchored' (by using NLP methods, for example) such that the light trance end-state can be achieved very quickly. Anymore I do pure meditation very rarely. Most of my work now is focused on my energy flow (see Uninhibited Energy Flow) and addressing any blockages that I might have.

> The goal of meditation, in regard to The Visceral Experience, is to reach a mild trance state. It is this trance state that creates the proper environment for energy to flow through your body.
>
> The end goal of improving your skills in maintained relaxation and light trance is to be able to pursue uninterrupted work toward gaining an uninhibited energy flow. I did not gain an understanding of my own energy flow until I had mastered and, to a certain extent, internalized the ability to fall quickly into a light trance. Once in the light trance, I was able to more quickly identify my internal energy as it eddied and flowed. And when I was able to identify it I was able to assert some control over the flow.

Energy Flow

Each of us has an innate energy flow which determines to a large extent how we experience our world and reality. Our energy flow can be healthy or unhealthy, restricted or unrestricted. The healthier and the less restricted this flow is, the healthier and happier we are. The more the world and reality seem to bend to our will even without effort.

The converse is true as well; the more restricted and unhealthy our energy flow then the more difficult our reality. We become emotionally and physically unwell. Obstacles present themselves to us at every opportunity. We suffer financially and mentally, and every day seems a struggle.

The goal of energy work is to ensure that our innate energy flow is unrestricted. This is a huge undertaking for many, because it entails working through emotional issues and traumas that have affected, and continue to affect, our daily lives. It is the emotional traumas that create the energy blocks, and it is the relief of those emotional traumas that will clear the blocks and allow energy to flow freely.

The first extension of this goal, for those who may already be there, is to strengthen our internal flow and clear out any remaining blockages.

> The second extension is to expand our energy flow beyond
> our own physical body to external objects and beings.

In Part III – Uninhibited Energy Flow I discuss this energy flow and detail a process for increasing it. The exercises listed will, as a by-product, help remove and overcome the blockages that are restricting your overall energy and causing physical and emotional illness.

Visualization

Visualization has been recognized for at least a century as being a method for interacting with reality. As a method to improve learning, memory and performance, it has proven invaluable. To be of real use, however, basic visualization must be improved upon and the results must become more consistent and replicable — methods for which I will discuss in Part III – Advanced Visualization.

The goal for the chapter on visualization is to learn how to create and use advanced visualizations, and what it is that separates the advanced from the standard.

Intention

Much talked about, but little understood, intention is the guiding light of The Visceral Experience. It is the strength or weakness of your intention that will determine the success of your psychic endeavor. In Part III – Powerful Intent, I will discuss how to determine and map out your current *true will*, so you know where you went wrong or right with past intentions. I will discuss setting goals, constructing affirmations and the overall process for producing the desired powerful intent.

The goal for the chapter on intention is to learn what constitutes a powerful intention and how to create one.

Daniel D. Barber

Reality

See Appendix A for discussions regarding **Theoretical Physics** and **Experiential Reality** .

Experiential Reality

Common sense tells us that the things of the earth exist only a little, and that true reality is only in dreams. ~Charles Baudelaire

Talking about theories only gets you so far. I do not cast aside my experiences as irrelevant just because they are not reproducible in a lab environment. My experience with psychic phenomena tells me there is far more to reality than science, religion or philosophy would have me believe, or can currently possibly explain. When I discuss my experiences later in Part IV – In Practice, I will also discuss their implications on the nature of reality.

My Understanding

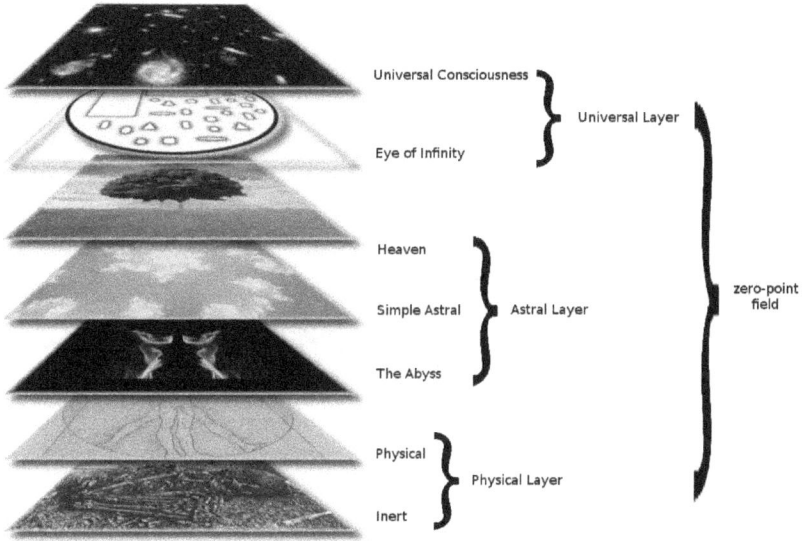

Universal Consciousness

Universal Layer

Eye of Infinity

Heaven

Simple Astral — Astral Layer

The Abyss

zero-point field

Physical

Physical Layer

Inert

Layers of Reality

The ideas I present that follow are, for lack of a better word, my theology. Together, they represent my view on the nature of reality based on both my understanding of theoretical physics and my personal experiences with altered states. As such my current understanding is dynamic and flexible, and I am certain will change as I experience more energy events. I'm presenting the following in the hopes that it will resonate with others who may have had similar experiences and perhaps shed some light on what they are going through.

The Zero-Point Field

In my experience the zero-point field is layer upon layer of frequencies coexisting within the same physical location. Each frequency layer within this field exhibits characteristics which I'll label according to my perception of their nature. There are seven frequencies, or realms, that I will be discussing. Starting from the bottommost I label them: The Inert, The Physical, The Abyss, The Simple Astral, Heaven, The Eye of Infinity, and The Universal Consciousness.

The Physical Layer

While we exist in all realms simultaneously, our physical presence, that which most of us consider to be real, exists within The Physical realm of The Physical Layer. Upon death, we pass into the lowest of the frequencies: The Inert.

The Astral Layer

The Abyss is the first level above The Physical Layer and is named as such due to its similarity to the occult idea of the same name, its easy confusion with our physical level, and the fear that can materialize there. The Simple Astral is above The

Abyss and is where free and fearless astral exploration generally takes place. And above that is Heaven which is the highest of the levels within The Astral Layer.

Heaven, as used here, is only a label named for the blissful characteristics of the experience. It should not be confused with the religious idea of an eternal resting place for lucky souls.

The Universal Layer

The Universal Layer is the topmost layer that I have experienced and consists of The Eye of Infinity at the lower frequency and the Universal Consciousness at the highest.

Of course the reality is without a doubt much more subtle, complex and extensive than my narrow experience would dictate. Still I feel it is illustrative to expound upon my experiences.

Please keep in mind that the preceding graphic depicts my experiences and how I conceive their relationship with each other and the zero-point field. Although I've used the word 'theology', I am not trying to start a religion.

Universal Consciousness

We are all a part of a Universal Consciousness at the highest frequencies of our being. This consciousness becomes more accessible to us as we dis-inhibit our innate energy and raise our vibrational rate. The Universal Consciousness is all-encompassing in its scope and is synonymous with the zero-point field of which everything is made and from which everything springs. This may be the 'Akashic Records' that we've all heard about — the library that holds the sum of all knowledge and wisdom of the universe.

Eye of Infinity

This is the experience I described in the introduction. It was similar in character to a standard OBE, but with one major difference: the control exhibited by the entity over my experience. I felt like I was a visitor to his reality, not like he was a part of mine.

Heaven

This is the top of The Astral Layer of experiences. Its character is blissful, happy and joyous, and it left within me a feeling of unity with all of mankind. I could see how others steeped in the religious thinking of their forefathers could interpret similar experiences as an expression of their particular heaven.

Simple Astral

The Simple Astral is the middle of The Astral Layer. It is in this layer that I became comfortable with the idea of altered states, with the idea that reality is not what is seems in waking life, and it is here that I learned some control over my out-of-body jaunts. This is the layer where William Buhlman spent the majority of his time and learned the mechanisms of control which he passed on in his book, *Adventures Beyond The Body*. This is where one can fly and pass through walls, visit friends and other planets. It is quite an extraordinary experience when you are able to wield some control over this state.

The Abyss

This is the lowest level in the astral layer and is situated, frequency-wise, right above waking reality. So close that the two can be difficult to differentiate. This is the level where our fears, worries, anxieties and perhaps neuroses run wild. It is called "the abyss" in esoteric occult writings because it is the primary obstacle one must overcome before proceeding to the higher levels. It is very easy to succumb to the fear that will present itself here. It is in this level where I believe hauntings and alien encounters occur.

Physical

This is the vibrational level occupied by humans, plants and animals — those things that exhibit a basic level of self-awareness. The physical is also a jail for those who don't explore beyond its limits.

Inert

This level consists of all of those materials which make up our perceived reality (the physical level), but which do not exhibit basic consciousness. The occupants of this level are earth in all of its various chemical makeups and the dead from the former occupants (humans, plants and animals) of the physical level.

Reality Summarized

The boundaries between us and each other, real as they are to
our limited perception, are all illusory.

If you can understand and accept the above assertion, you will be on the road to powerfully using The Visceral Experience. You will start to look at life and your interactions with others differently. You will no longer consider reacting to others with violence, anger or aggression. Visiting harm on others is to harm The Universal Consciousness — and you are The Universal Consciousness! In effect you are damaging yourself every time you lose your temper.

Conversely, helping others benefits the Universal Consciousness (yourself) and, in fact, simply avoiding conflict is a move in a positive direction. Doing so habitually makes it easier and easier to do so in the future.

I have always enjoyed being able to do a good deed, but now I will go even further out of my way to help others in any way possible. By no means am I perfect in this regard and will sometimes let my hurt feelings or anger interfere with how I should act. I have however made incredible strides since the selfishness of my youth and as I work on silencing my ego-based reactions, I continue to make progress on improving my kindness and helpfulness. Proactively doing good and helping others creates positive change in the world, influences those you help to do the same, and feels great! It creates happiness and thankfulness which are two qualities that are severely lacking in today's world.

What you must realize, understand and accept is that we, even in our physical form, are made of photons and are pure energy. We are *all* simply manifestations of a singular source: the zero-point field. *Everything* is an energetic manifestation of that singular source. There exists nothing but energy in different forms with different attributes. All that exists is energy and *we are all one*.

This book is littered with quotes from ancient philosophers regarding their observations and sometimes surreal interpretations of reality. But it is also instructive to look at what modern physicists had to say about reality. These are men, dedicated and rigorous scientists each, who spent days immersed in mathematical calculation and their entire lives trying to understand the enigma that is the subatomic world. No one would ever accuse them of being head-in-the-cloud new-age hippies.

And yet some of their beliefs could be confused with that of the most philosophical of philosophers, or the most progressive of hallucinogenic drug users! Read the following quotes while keeping in mind the boundary-less nature of reality.

Albert Einstein

- "Mass and energy are both but different manifestations of the same thing."
- "Reality is merely an illusion, albeit a very persistent one."
- "As far as the laws of mathematics refer to reality, they are not certain, and as far as they are certain, they do not refer to reality."
- "We still do not know one thousandth of one percent of what nature has revealed to us."
- "The world as we have created it is a process of our thinking. It cannot be changed without changing our thinking."

Werner Heisenberg

- "I think that modern physics has definitely decided in favor of Plato. In fact the smallest units of matter are not physical objects in the ordinary sense; they are forms, ideas which can be expressed unambiguously only in mathematical language."
- "The atom of modern physics can only be symbolized by a partial differential equation in an abstract multidimensional space."

Niels Bohr

- "If quantum mechanics hasn't profoundly shocked you, you haven't understood it yet."
- "Isolated material particles are abstractions, their properties being definable and observable only through their interaction with other systems."
- "We are all agreed that your theory is crazy. The question that divides us is whether it is crazy enough to have a chance of being correct."
- "Everything we call real is made of things that cannot be regarded as real."

Erwin Schrodinger

- "Quantum physics thus reveals a basic oneness of the universe."
- "A careful analysis of the process of observation in atomic physics has shown that the subatomic particles have no meaning as isolated entities, but can only be understood as interconnections between the preparation of an experiment and the subsequent measurement."
- "What we observe as material bodies and forces are nothing but shapes and variations in the structure of space."

Max Born

- "The belief that there is only one truth and that oneself is in possession of it seems to me the root of all the evil that is in the world."
- "I am now convinced that theoretical physics is actually philosophy."

Louis De Broglie

- "The actual state of our knowledge is always provisional and... there must be, beyond what is actually known, immense new regions to discover."

Max Planck

- "I regard consciousness as fundamental. I regard matter as derivative from consciousness. We cannot get behind consciousness. Everything that we talk about, everything that we regard as existing, postulates consciousness."
- "As a man who has devoted his whole life to the most clear headed science, to the study of matter, I can tell you as a result of my research about atoms this much: There is no matter as such. All matter originates and exists only by virtue of a force which brings the particle of an atom to vibration and holds this most minute solar system of the atom together. We must assume behind this force the existence of a conscious and intelligent mind. This mind is the matrix of all matter."

Interacting With The Quantum

Okay, so The Quantum is this amazing place where reality is flexible and changes depending upon circumstance, intent and expectation. Great. *What does that have to do with me?*

Absolutely everything.

Scientists don't like that answer because of the great difference in size between you and a photon, but the reality of it is that you are made of atoms and those atoms constitute your brain, your spine and your gut. Every feeling, emotion, urge, and annoyance you experience is also experienced by each atom in your body. And those atoms communicate directly with The Quantum. The Quantum (alternatively the zero-point field or The Universal Consciousness) will act upon that communication — sometimes subtly and sometimes not so subtly depending upon the intensity and duration of your feelings and desires.

Physicists, while completely at ease with theorizing extra dimensions in order to make their mathematical constructs work, would nonetheless argue against the simplicity of the above assertion. Regardless, my reasoning is beyond question. Atoms are a part of The Quantum. Our bodies are composed of atoms. Because we are unable to direct individual atoms to do our bidding does not mean that we cannot create the proper circumstance for encouraging The Quantum to do what we want it to do. This takes training and dedication, but is completely possible. It is not easy, necessarily, but possible.

What About Consciousness?

In the double-slit experiment photons exhibited control over their environment by choosing which slit to travel through. What role then does consciousness, the atom's or ours, play in the decisions made by photons?

It is impossible to separate the intentions and expectations of the experimenter from the observed results; those intentions and expectations are reflected in the placement of the measuring device, type of device chosen and the choice of what is being measured.

In this context, intent and expectation are simply different words for consciousness. To clarify: the observer's *conscious* intent and *conscious* expectation have an effect on the observed results. The consciousness of the observer is, through the choices the experimenter makes, thereby transferred to the experiment and must therefore be regarded as part of the equation when considering the effect on the path and behavior of the photon in flight.

This force of intent and the consciousness behind it is part of the function that creates reality from The Quantum potential. This is the basis for the Law of Attraction.

Reality

If you take anything away from reading this book, please let it be this. This understanding of reality is so fundamental to making positive changes in your life that I cannot stress it enough.

- Energy and mass are both attributes of a single primal object. Energy is a form of mass, and vice-versa. This primal object, in all of its various forms as energy or mass, is all there is. We know it variously as the zero-point field, The Universal Consciousness or The Quantum.

- The zero-point field is omnipresent and all-pervasive; it exists everywhere and in everything, from inside each of your cells to the farthest extent of the universe. It is a field of pure potential energy, each photon of which is waiting to be called into existence by intent. Everything is pure potential at the subatomic level.

- Every atom in our body interacts with The Quantum on a continual basis; we are not separate from The Quantum. We subconsciously and continuously interface with The Universal Consciousness through subatomic, or quantum, action. Every intent, expectation and feeling we have creates a reaction within our cells and thereby within The Quantum by collapsing potential into reality.

- The zero-point field is made up of different frequencies which correspond to different perceptions of reality. These range from The Universal Consciousness to The Inert (See previous discussion on Experiential Reality). Inhabitants of these various levels are limited in perception to their current level and the levels below. It is through spiritual work that higher levels can be perceived and attained.

- One attribute of energy is consciousness. The zero-point field, this mass of omnipresent energetic potential, is conscious though perhaps to a degree that we are incapable of perceiving or understanding.

- Life is a synonym for consciousness.

- Life and consciousness are continuous and unending.

- Though difficult, it is possible to consciously and effectively interface with The Quantum. One accomplishes this through a combination of innate energetic ability, advanced visualization and powerful intention — in other words, by using The Visceral Experience.

Utilizing This New Understanding

It is one thing to have an intellectual understanding of the above stated characteristics of reality, and another entirely to fully accept them when they are in complete disagreement with everything you perceive. How can you accept that there are no boundaries in reality when your senses tell you that the table beneath your hand is solid? How can you feel the texture of that cushion sitting on the couch across the room when your arms reach only so far? How can you feel what that person is feeling when that person is separate from you?

The simple answer is that you must force the process along by using your imagination to expand your perception. Instead of seeing a solidly physical table beneath your hand you can shift your mental gears and view it as a collection of atoms which are loosely bound by magnetic fields. In reality the amount of nothingness in the table far exceeds its mass. It is this 'nothingness' in everything that exists with which you should strive to interact.

Instead of seeing the distance between yourself and that cushion across the room, focus on the 'nothingness' that is in between. With a conscious shift, view that 'nothingness' as a latent field of energetic potential. Energetic potential permeates

Daniel D. Barber

everything, the cushion and yourself included, and knows no boundaries. Neither should you. Imagine reaching out with your energy and touching the cushion. Feel the texture of the cushion beneath your energetic fingertips. Instead of seeing a separate person sitting across from you, endeavor to see another facet of yourself.

The more you practice this process of ignoring perceptual boundaries, the more you will be able to work around them.

Requisite Skills

Daniel D. Barber

Overview

Imagination creates reality. ~Richard Wagner

Please be aware that if you are pregnant, have heart problems or are in general ill-health, it is not advisable to attempt the following exercises. As a result of my work with energy, I have experienced significant heart palpitations and only continued my work after consulting with a doctor and receiving a stamp of approval.

A true understanding of The Visceral Experience, like many mental skills, requires practice, practice and more practice. It requires success, it requires failure, it requires effort and diligence and introspection. And it requires at least a partial mastery of the requisite skill-sets which follow.

This chapter will address each of these skills in detail and will include exercises for each that will enable you to progress from novice to skilled user. The end of each section will include the goal and desired result for the skill-set.

Maintained Relaxation

Do the difficult things while they are easy and do the great things while they are small. A journey of a thousand miles must begin with a single step. ~Lao Tzu

Relaxation is one of two bedrock skills that the whole structure of The Visceral Experience is built upon. The ability to relax and to be relaxed is integral to successful meditation, which is integral to learning about your internal energy and other aspects of yourself. Even advanced practitioners such as myself must maintain a relaxed state in order to practice and grow in The Visceral Experience.

The following exercises will provide a basic and increasingly more challenging path for gaining your own mastery of relaxation.

The Out Breath

The space between exhale and inhale is where the body is at its most quiet. It is in this space that you can check in with the heartbeat and truly feel what is happening with your body — it is here that you will notice the various tensions and can consciously mitigate those discomforts as they rise into your awareness. This is the space where true relaxation happens.

Counting Breaths

Assume a relaxed position whether it be lying down, reclining in your favorite chair, or sitting in your favorite yoga pose, and breathe in deeply for a count of four. Without holding your breath at the top of the cycle, begin to exhale at a comfortable pace for a count of four. Continue this cycle until this process is as easy and strain-free as possible. Extend the count as long as you wish, keeping it consistent for both inhale and exhale.

A slightly more advanced version is to add a pause at the bottom and top of the breath cycle. For example, after an inhale of four counts, hold the breath in for a count of two, then exhale for a count of four and rest for a count of two before inhaling again. It is in the quiet of the empty lungs where true relaxation occurs. Extend the count to your capability and comfort level.

Toes Up

This is the most basic of relaxation exercises and it can be found in pretty much every book regarding relaxation or meditation. To start, clench all of the muscles in your feet for a count of two and then relax. Move up and do the same with your calves, thighs, pelvic area and buttocks, abdomen, chest, arms, hands, neck and face. At the end of this exercise, the common wisdom is that you'll be relaxed. I've never liked this method and generally found it to be far too much work and neither enjoyable nor relaxing. I include it here simply in the interest of completeness.

The Sphincter

I know, I know. But we have to talk about it. The sphincter and the associated muscles in the lower abdomen and buttocks are by far the most important muscles to relax. In my experience, when my sphincter is relaxed (not messily of course), my body is relaxed. It seems to be the last muscle to truly relax. In fact, I am to the point now that if I am running energy through my body and I am not totally relaxed, my sphincter will relax of its own accord. I am surprised every time that happens as I would be thinking that I was already in a relaxed state.

Sinking Mantra

This exercise could also be considered a meditation and is actually a powerful tool, in combination with other factors, for attaining OBE. While lying on your back mentally repeat the mantra "relax" with each exhale as you feel yourself sinking into the bed. Your breath should be slow, comfortable and not strained in any way. If discomfort arises acknowledge it and discard it without effort and return quickly to your relaxed mantra. After a while you may begin to feel like your body has become a shell and notice subtle energy effects such as a disassociation from your extremities to the point you can't really tell where they are or how they are situated.

Relaxation End State

Relaxation is a stepping stone to better meditation, which is another step towards recognizing and building your innate energetic ability. You should be able to immediately recognize when your mind and body enter a relaxed state. This is more difficult than it may seem; as I mentioned earlier, I will be running energy when my muscles will spontaneously relax of their own accord. Clearly this identifies running energy is another way to achieve relaxation, but that puts the cart before the horse. Being relaxed before running energy makes the whole process tons easier and is a good habit to get into.

Light Trance

To the mind that is still, the whole universe surrenders. ~Lao
Tzu

Meditation, together with a solid base of maintained relaxation, is necessary to allowing your energy to flow in an uninhibited manner. A trance, typified by a feeling of lightness, floating and detachment, signals success in meditation and lets you know that you are ready to begin energy work.

For any type of psychic practice, it is helpful to put yourself into a relaxed state of awareness — an awareness of your internal state as well as your external circumstances. I find that I practice energy work best at night as I am getting ready to go to sleep. I lie on my back with my hands at my side, on my thighs or above my head. In the following meditation exercises use whichever position most allows you to meditate freely.

I don't know if this distinction has ever been made, but I like to think of meditation as being one of two types: active or passive. Passive meditation, like the Empty Mind exercise presented shortly, is where you try to empty your mind of all distracting thoughts in the manner of Zen or Buddhist meditation.

Daniel D. Barber

For me, this type of meditation is the most difficult although it is
potentially also the most rewarding. Active meditation, as
described in the rest of the exercises, is where you choose
something to focus on and study to the exclusion of all other
sensory inputs. With this type of meditation, I've had nothing but
success and it has led me to greater and greater insights and
capabilities. I'll give several examples of active meditation with
which I've experienced success.

Of course, there are multitudes of books on meditation,
relaxation methods and self-hypnosis available to you. If the
methods I propose below don't resonate with you, find those
books and methods that work for you and practice until you have
mastered the technique.

Empty Mind

After relaxing your body by whichever method works
best for you, empty your mind of all thoughts. Your mind will
wander and at times you'll notice your everyday worries popping
up and causing your body to tense. Once you notice this
happening, allow those everyday thoughts to dissipate without
rebuking yourself, and resume your mindlessness. Physical
discomforts will also prove to be another serious distraction.
After a while in any pose, you may notice some soreness, or an

itch or a tickle. Acknowledge and recognize this discomfort, make adjustments as necessary, and immediately move your mind back into a clear state. Maintain this state as long as you can.

Breath Focus

Find your relaxed space and focus on your breath. Try to breathe slow and deep without making the exercise laborious. Feel your chest rise and lower as you breathe; with each exhale feel yourself sink into the earth. Continue to focus on your breath. Like the Empty Mind exercise, observe your discomforts and distractions; recognize and discard them.

Heart Focus

Find your relaxed space and focus on your heartbeat. Use your heartbeat to measure breaths, inhaling for so many heartbeats and exhaling for the same count. Use the same methods for dealing with distractions and discomforts as with the previous exercises. Advanced practitioners might count a heartbeat or two between inhales and exhales. This is a very effective meditation and will get you to a trance state quickly. The more intensely focused on your heartbeat, the deeper the meditation.

Follow The Spot

This is perhaps my favorite of all the meditations and I believe it is one of the most effective. Taking slow, deep breaths and observing your body is the best place to start. Become aware of the tensions and sore spots in your body. Direct your attention to those points and simply observe. You will find that the sore spot you set your attention on will slowly melt away allowing a new spot elsewhere on your body to rise to your attention. Focus on the new spot until it too melts away; repeat the process until you find you have reached a highly pleasurable trance state. Try to maintain this state as long as possible. This is also a self-healing method and works wonderfully.

Trance End State

Practice with meditation, in combination with a steady state of relaxation, should allow one to fall quickly into a light trance. The light trance state is the prerequisite for skillful and powerful use of one's innate energy.

Uninhibited Energy Flow

It is folly for a man to pray to the gods for that which he has the power to obtain by himself. ~Epicurus

Energy work is the primary foundation which supports not only The Visceral Experience, but also the two skills of powerful intention and advanced visualization. Every person has internal energy available to them for use in interacting with reality. The stronger, deeper and more disciplined your use of this energy, the more effective the intention and visualization will be and thus the more powerful The Visceral Experience. If your internal energy is weak or undisciplined the end result will be equally weak and undisciplined. Everything rests on the foundation of your own internal energy flow.

Internal Energy Work

Having the ability to perceive and feel your own internal energy is a prerequisite for being able to successfully create a visceral experience. The subtle perception required when recognizing and working with your internal energy is the same depth of attention required when utilizing The Visceral Experience.

Daniel D. Barber

As noted in the previous discussion on reality, we are energy. The fact that your physical body is a solid form of energy does not preclude other energy from flowing though you. Your heart is regulated by electrical impulses and your thoughts themselves are the result of electrical impulses between synapses in your brain.

Numerous frameworks have been created throughout the centuries to help people understand and interact with the energy inherent in every person's body. The energy is variously termed chi, ki, qi, or kundalini by different cultures with frameworks as diverse as chakras, meridians, subtle energy body, auras, etc. Each of these frameworks are legitimate descriptions of the human energy system described initially by folks who experienced human energy in that particular way. They are not exclusive from each other nor are they the only methods for experiencing and exploring the human energy system. They are, however, useful starting points for beginners. I started by exploring the chakra system and find the term 'subtle energy body' to be fairly accurate in its connotations, though I will use the term more generally here.

Humans are more than the physical body that we inhabit on this physical plane. Of this there is no question. Less intrusive on our attention, of course, is our subtle energy body which we cart around part and parcel with our physical body. The purpose then of energy work is to pour as much attention into developing our innate energy ability (our subtle energy body) as we do in developing our physical body, our intellect or our skill-sets.

The benefits of exploring the subtle energy body are numerous. For the diligent person it is possible, with practice and patience, to increase the amount of energy flowing unrestricted within. This improved energy flow will have a noticeable positive effect on physical, mental and emotional health. Various 'psychic' skills will begin to manifest and can be developed by continued energy work and practice of the specific skill-set that is of interest. Throughout my growth in energetic ability I have explored out-of-body experiences, the ability to heal with energy, the ability to induce somatic reactions in others with my mind (energetic projection) and other, less noticeable effects.

I will discard the various mystical and esoteric terms and concepts that have grown hand-in-hand with these frameworks over the centuries in favor of a straightforward and clear description of the basic concepts. It is without these obfuscating terms that I was successful in learning these frameworks.

Daniel D. Barber

Breath Work

Breath work is very powerful and could be considered a bridge between pure meditation and energy work, as it encompasses elements of both. Breath work, called pranayama in the yogic tradition, consists of various breathing techniques sometimes in combination with the clenching or relaxation of various groups of muscles.

When I do practice, I am more likely to engage with breath work rather than pure meditation. With breath work I can manipulate my energy flow which helps with finding and clearing obstacles.

> The goal of breath work is to both quiet the mind and to begin to become familiar with your body's energy system.

The Deep Breath

The ability to breathe fully and deeply is essential to a good practice. In a relaxed position, whether it be laying down or sitting in a yoga pose, inhale slowly while expanding your belly allowing the breath to fill the lower parts of your lungs to capacity. Continue to inhale until your belly fills to capacity and the breath fills the upper part of your lungs expanding your chest. Exhale naturally and without effort. Repeat this four times at a minimum, eight times for medium effect and 12 times to truly stir your energy.

Breath of Fire

Sitting on your knees with your buttocks resting on your feet, quickly and strongly pull your stomach into your spine, forcing all of the air out of your lungs. Then, relax those muscles, allowing your belly to expand and lungs to fill passively with air. And again. Repeat this cycle as fast as you can, starting with a thirty second practice and slowly increasing to two minutes or whatever you feel is appropriate. Consistent practice with this exercise will increase the vibrational rate of your entire subtle energy body.

Energy Pump

From any position in which you are comfortable, come to a relaxed cycle of breathing. In conjunction with your next exhale, tense your buttocks, genital and lower abdomen muscles. Then, relax all of your muscles and inhale. Repeat this cycle until you feel a burning in your solar plexus chakra. This exercise really primes your center chakra and will provide abundant energy to whatever you attempt next. Do not try this exercise at night before bed — you will not sleep.

Yoga

Yoga originated as a method to remove distractions from meditation. Some guy a long time ago said, "I bet if I stretch before sitting down to meditate, I'll be bothered less by muscle cramps, etc." He was right. Since then, yoga has diverged into two different paths: the physical and the energetic. Many yogas tend to be just about physical capability, which is exactly the purpose it was intended for. Doing hatha yoga is not an end in and of itself, it is simply a tool to allow one to meditate with less distraction. Kundalini yoga, however, evolved to incorporate breath work and muscle locks — both of which function to ramp up your internal energy. After a session of Kundalini, you will likely feel physically tired yet energetically *ramped up* at the same time. Kundalini is really much more like calisthenics than what you usually think about when you think about yoga. It is very focused on a specific outcome and is not necessarily pretty to watch.

> Kundalini yoga is a means to an end and is not the goal itself. Some have made a religion out of it. Do not get trapped into thinking that's all there is.

Chakras

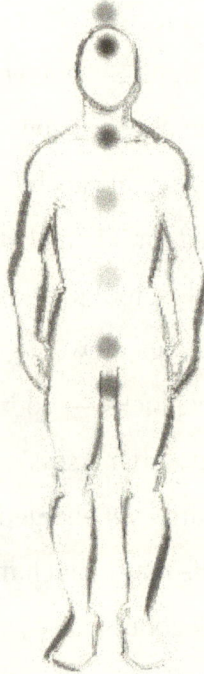

Chakra Framework

The chakra system, in its simplest form, consists of seven points on a person's physical body where it is easiest to feel the human energy system. It is as if the human energy system somehow comes to the surface at these points. By concentrating your attention at these points and manipulating via various visualizations, you can excite the energy latent within and begin to feel and experience the subtle energy body.

The major chakras, as depicted in the illustration, are:

- Root (according to most sources, located at or near the perineum).

- Sacral (again, according to most sources, this is between the pubic bone and slightly below the belly button. I have felt it in a variety of places in that area).

- Solar Plexus (where the ribs come together, but slightly lower).

- Heart (located in center of chest; really should be called the thymus chakra, as it is located directly over that particular gland).

- Throat (anywhere from Adam's apple to top of collar bones).

- Third Eye (between, and slightly above, the eyebrows).

- Crown (top of the head; I feel mine most strongly in my skull, directly above my spine).

Chakra Associations: Frequently included in books that describe chakras are lists of different associations, such as color, sound, emotion, connection to internal organs, etc. for each chakra. Some of these associations I've experienced and tested and some I have not; and some, I think, are the remnants of age-old mysticism.

I can attest to some of the emotional associations of the chakras, and as I mentioned when describing The Eye of Infinity, I associated the color orange with the shaft of energy that shot up my spine. Other attributes, such as the sound and color of each chakra, I have not experienced but don't necessarily discount. However, part of the purpose of this book is to remove the mysticism from what is really a fairly straightforward process. Therefore I will only write about what I have experienced.

As an example of age-old mysticism that over-complicates and confuses, the crown chakra (Sahasrara in Sanskrit) is depicted as a thousand-petaled lotus associated with the color white or violet. It has a symbol and a mantra and is associated with "inner wisdom and the death of the body [and] connects to the central nervous system via the hypothalamus"[1]. Although I might agree with some of the associations, I disagree with others and recommend to everyone using the chakra framework to rely on their own experience.

---

1   http://en.wikipedia.org/wiki/Chakras#Description_of_the_chakras

Daniel D. Barber

Exercises

The illustrations below will use a cycling green, blue, red and yellow to illustrate the movement of energy, attention or consciousness as described in the accompanying exercise. Green will always be the start point..

Hands and Feet:

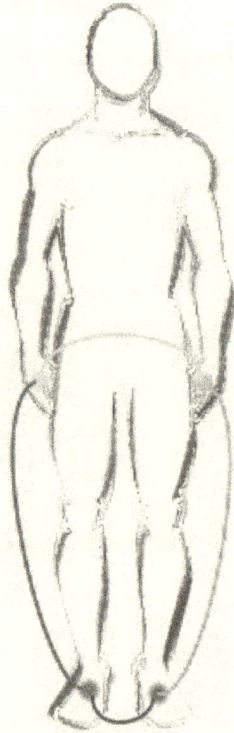

Hands and Feet

This is a simple exercise in focusing your attention, but is also helpful in learning to feel your energy. First, focus your attention on the palm of your left hand. Keep your attention there until you feel your palm tingling slightly. Then move your

Daniel D. Barber

attention to the sole of your left foot. Again, concentrate there until you feel the bottom of your foot tingling. Now to your right foot. Same thing; when the bottom of that foot is tingling, move your awareness to the palm of your right hand. Continue this exercise until you are able to simultaneously feel your awareness in both hands and both feet.

Hands and Feet Speeding:

Start with the Hands and Feet exercise. When you have successfully brought awareness to all four extremities at the same time, begin to move your attention, *as fast as you can* from left hand to left foot to right foot to right hand. Be sure not to let your imagination outrun your awareness. Make sure that as you move from extremity to extremity, you pause long enough to actually *feel* the tingling sensation. This will seem to take a long time at first, but the more you practice, the better able you will be to focus your attention quickly.

Hands and Feet Traveling:

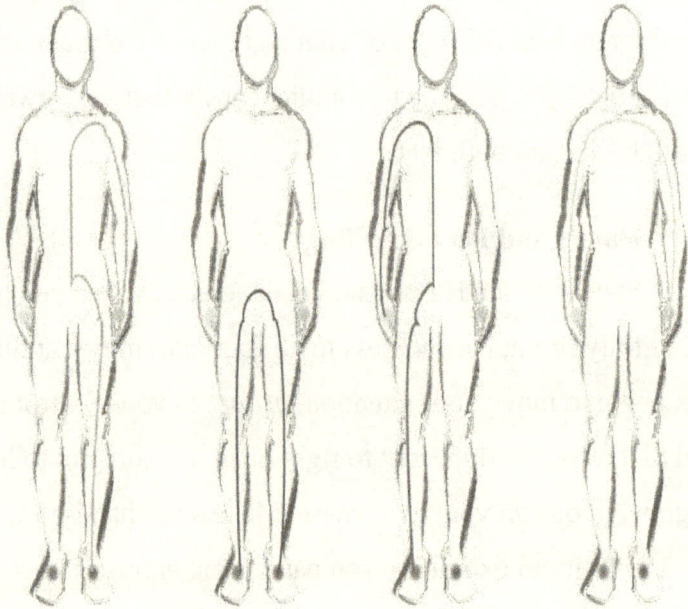

Hands and Feet Traveling

Again, start with the basic exercise, but this time try to feel the energy as it travels from extremity to extremity. Experience the energy as it moves from your left palm, up your arm, into your heart chakra, down your spine, down your left leg and finally into the sole of your left foot. Let your attention settle there for a moment until the sole of your left foot is tingling strongly. Then, experience the energy as it moves up your left calf and thigh, into your sacral or root chakra and then down your right leg and into your right foot. Now, experience the energy as it flows up your right leg into your root chakra, up your spine into your heart chakra, down into your right arm and into the palm of your right hand. And, lastly, feel the energy as it moves up your right arm, into your heart chakra, into your left arm and down, to complete the circuit, into your left palm again.

Once you have the hang of this exercise, try to see how fast you can go with it, all the while maintaining a focused attention on the energy.

Another variation:

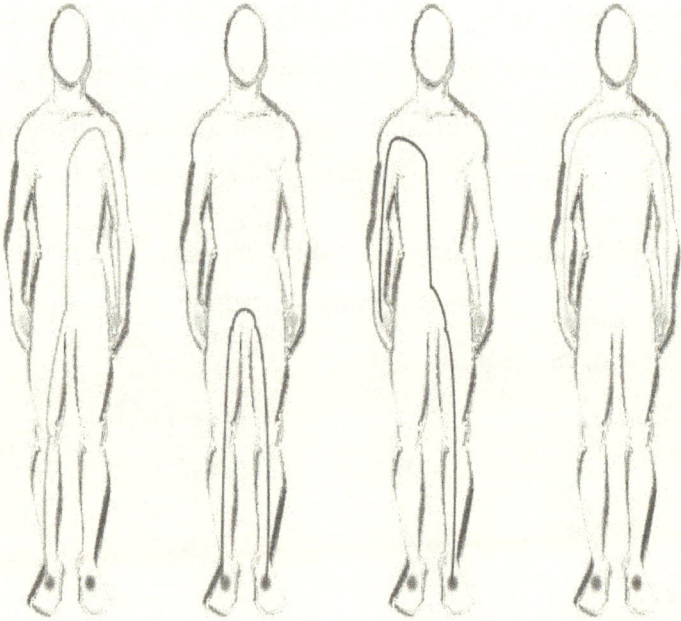

Hands and Feet Traveling (crisscross)

Move the energy in a crisscross pattern from left hand to right foot, right foot to right hand, right hand to left foot. Try to move this pattern as fast as you can. Be aware that, if you stand up after, you may not be able to walk straight.

Advanced:

Hands and Feet Traveling (cross the midline)

Stir up both left hand and left foot, then bounce that energy across your center to your right hand and right foot at the same time. Go back and forth and see how fast you can make it happen.

Breathing Through the Chakra:

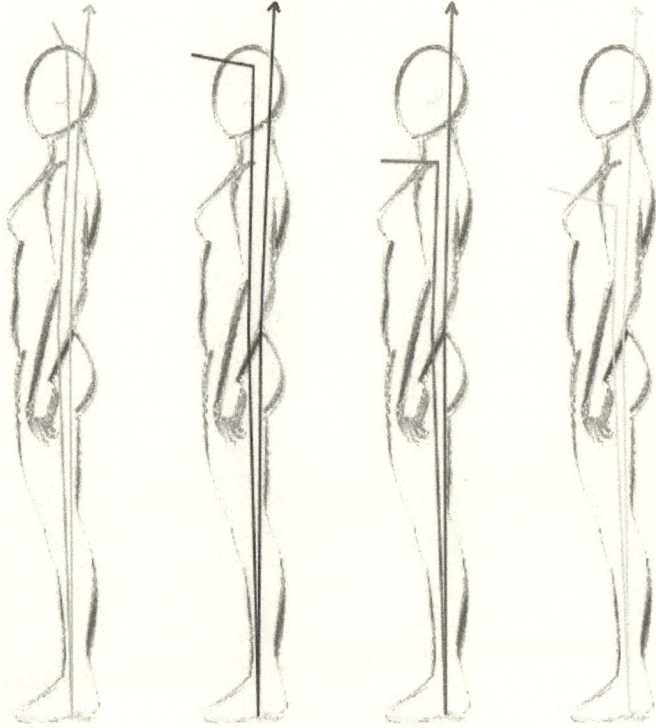

Breathing Through Chakras

Envision a translucent tube at your crown chakra and, with your natural, relaxed inhale, imagine oxygen, the stuff of life, entering your body through this tube. Feel the oxygen enter your head, travel down your spine all the way to the soles of your feet. With your natural, relaxed exhale, the oxygen returns from your feet, travels up your legs and spine and exits through your crown chakra. Breathe in, in order, with each of your chakras, always exhaling through your crown. As you get to your lower chakras, you may want to change the flow such that your breath travels up to your heart and pause there before exiting through the crown. Repeat this exercise at each chakra until you can feel the chakra spinning.

Connecting the Chakras:

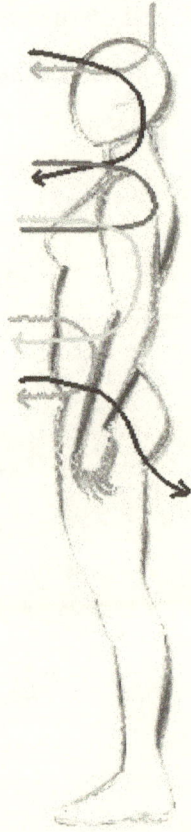

Connecting Chakras

This is an extension of the previous exercise, following the same general methodology with the tubes. This time, however, once you feel the chakra spinning, exhale through the next chakra down or up, depending on the direction you are traveling. For example, start at your root chakra, breathe in and out until you feel the energy there. Then, instead of stopping and starting at the next chakra, you inhale one last time through the root chakra and then exhale through your sacral chakra. Then you breathe in and out through your sacral chakra until you feel the energy spinning there. Continue until you have spun up your crown chakra.

Point to Point:

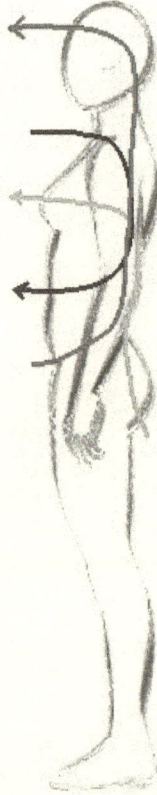

Point to Point

This is a slightly more advanced practice that you may want to try after spinning up your chakras through the previous two exercises. Again, with the tubes, breathe in through a chakra of your choice and send the energy down to your feet, but this time exhale through a different chakra, doing so until you feel the energy coursing between the two. Once that connection is strong create a connection between two others (your choice) and repeat the process. Travel the chakras, connecting and energizing them. You can pick chakras randomly or travel from the crown down, or the root up.

Spinning the Ball:

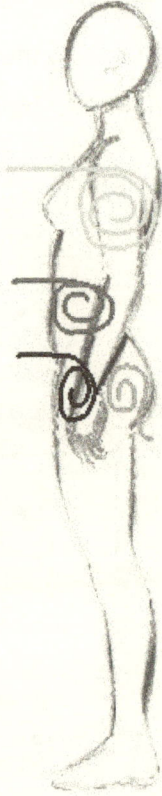

Spinning the Ball

    Once you gain some level of mastery over the above method, you may want to dispose of the image of the tube, as it can be limiting once you're beyond the basics. With this exercise, you breathe in through your root chakra, such that your breath travels into your body very close to the inside of your spine. Then you imagine that breath curling into a ball towards the front of your body. Keep that ball spinning there as long as you can, through multiple breaths. Use your inhales to give the spinning ball momentum. You can do this exercise with each chakra individually. The image below depicts the first four cycles (green, blue, red, yellow) of this exercise. Continue on until you've hit all seven major chakras.

Spinning Through Multiple Chakras:

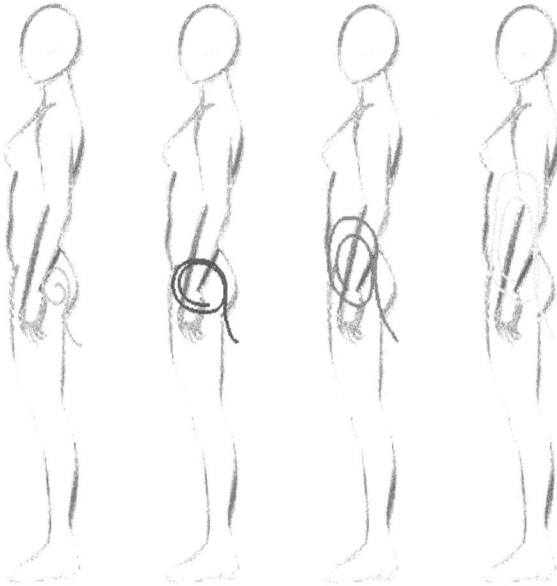

Spinning Through Multiple Chakras

This exercise is an expansion on Spinning the Ball. You start out the same by breathing through your root chakra on the inside of your spine. Once the root chakra is spinning, include your sacral chakra: breathe in as normal and on exhale increase the size of the ball until it includes your sacral chakra. Once the sacral is spun up, increase the size of the ball until it includes your solar plexus — and so on and so forth up through the rest of the chakras. This is a pretty amazing exercise and at the end of it, with this vortex of energy spinning through your entire body, you will feel like you're in another reality.

Daniel D. Barber

Drawing on the Wall:

One of my challenges as I've increased my energy flow has been the pressure-like headaches I would get when moving energy up into my crown chakra. It almost seemed as though the energy would hit the inside of my skull and would get trapped there. The standard visualization for moving past this type of block is the lotus flower gently unfolding its petals. That didn't work for me — possibly because lotus flowers are not an ingrained part of American culture like they are in India, i.e., they have no inherent meaning to me. It's great imagery and beautiful, but pretty worthless in my case. I had to find another way.

When I first did this, it helped to be lying on my back in bed, the headboard or wall right 'above' me. Start a rotation of energy, just the outside of a circle around the top of your head. Once you have that going well, imagine an arm and a hand extending from the circumference of that circle (the dotted line in the illustration below), holding a pencil and drawing a circle on the wall above you. Really *feel* as the pencil meets the wall and the lead is transferred. This seemed to open up my crown and release me from those headaches.

Subtle Energy Body

Drawing on the Wall

Increased awareness of one's own subtle energy body is a natural consequence of increasing one's internal energy through the use of chakra work or one of the other energy-working frameworks. But the goal of all of these systems should be removing, or moving beyond, the restriction of specific frameworks. This is an important goal in gaining a complete awareness of your body's energy system. I consider the "subtle energy body" to be a descriptive term for the energy body as a whole. Chakras and meridians and all of the other frameworks are a good starting point for learning about your energy body, but true mastery cannot be gained without an understanding of the whole. Once you have moved beyond the starting point of the chakra or meridian system, you will become aware that the limitations expressed by those frameworks no longer exist. For instance, instead of spinning up a single chakra because it corresponds to a particular aspect of your being (intellect, love, etc), you will simply spin up your entire energy body. Spinning up the entire energy body as a whole has the effect of evening out energy imbalances that cause various illnesses. It is also, as you might surmise, very powerful. The following exercises will help you to move beyond those artificial boundaries.

Expanding / Retracting:

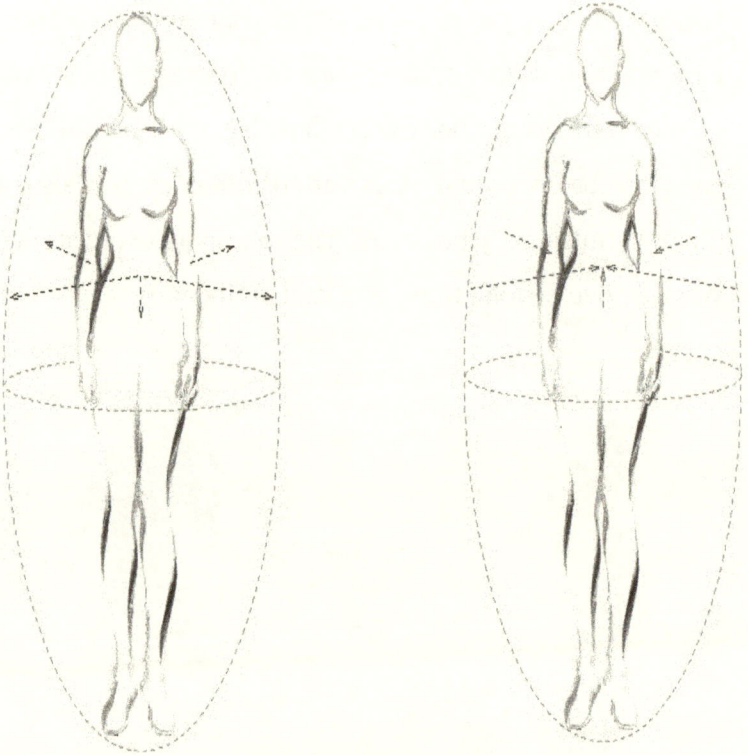

Expanding / Retracting

This exercise is more of a whole body practice and
requires you forget, for the most part, the whole concept of
chakras though they are still useful as points of reference. For
me, this exercise seems to be particularly effective for gaining a
peaceful relaxation and a wider perspective on the world.
Imagine yourself on the inside of an invisible ball of energy just
big enough to stand up in. With an exhale (this might seem

89

Daniel D. Barber

backwards, but it is the natural inclination once you get the imagery down), bring all of this energy in and collapse it into your subtle energy body through your solar plexus chakra. With your next inhale blow that energy back into this invisible shell of energy all around you. Once you're doing this right it will almost feel like there is some resistance to pulling the energy back into your solar plexus — as if the outward racing energy actually has momentum that you need to stop and pull back in.

Advanced I:

Repeat this exercise using each of the seven chakras as the focal point. Make sure that you consciously follow and feel the energy as you move it for a powerful effect.

More Advanced:

When you pull the energy back into whichever chakra you are using as the focal point, imagine that it spins into a vortex within your body and reaches down to your spine.

90

Super Advanced:

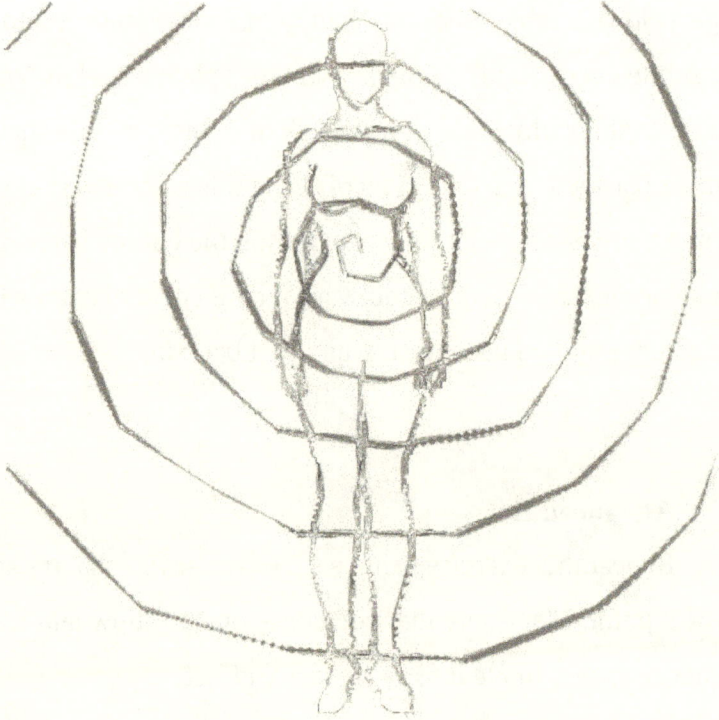

Expanding / Retracting into Vortex

When you pull the energy back in, pull it back in to a spot outside of your body or into someone else's.

Super Duper Advanced:

Expand the energetic globe as far out as you can, place your consciousness there and look back down at yourself. This seems to be a good method for learning remote viewing, as I've been able to look down on my house and even on my city.

Daniel D. Barber

The Healing Circuit:

The Healing Circuit

Lying on your back, place your hands on your thighs with your elbows slightly away from your body. Smoothly flow your energy down your left arm, across your hand to your thigh, through your sacral chakra, up your right arm into your spine at the back of your neck (throat chakra), and back down your left arm. Run this circuit slowly until you can easily feel the moving energy. Speed up the rotation.

Advanced:

Increase the size until the circuit envelopes your whole body from feet to head and beyond. This is a very powerful activity and when done correctly will energize your entire subtle energy body all by itself. This exercise is likely one that will be used primarily by advanced energy work practitioners because the amount of energy that needs to be moved is fairly massive.

Advanced:

Tie off the flow so that it will move without your direct attention. You should be able to relax your focus, let your mind wander and then find the flow moving easily when you return your attention to it.

Neuro-Linguistic Programming (NLP)

Neuro-Linguistic Programming is an amazing advance in understanding the mind. It is the study of human learning — what works, what doesn't, and methods for maximizing a person's ability to learn. I am by no means an expert in NLP. I have only pulled from it the pieces that I have found interesting and useful to me in my endeavors with energy work, meditation and hypnosis.

The first book I read on the subject was the book by Michael Brooks called *Instant Rapport.* It was marketed toward sales professionals and the "How To" crowd. I think I've also found it in the psychology aisle. Rapport is defined as a "connection, especially harmonious or sympathetic relation" between two people. And establishing rapport, at least when you are first starting out, is the first step in initiating an energetic projection. One of the best ways to establish rapport with another person is to mirror their actions.

Basic Mirroring:

Next time you are at lunch with a co-worker give basic mirroring a try. The process is simple enough — to initiate rapport with someone, simply copy their actions. You don't have to mimic them exactly; a general imitation of their movements and behavior will suffice. If that person picks up a drink you pick up the salt. If they scratch their ear you touch your chin. Your mirroring should be casual and calm — do not overdue it! Mirroring too closely or too quickly will break rapport and leave both of you feeling a bit awkward. With this basic exercise, work on establishing and maintaining rapport without swinging too many times between rapport and discomfort.

Breath Mirroring:

Mirroring another person's breathing is a very powerful method for establishing rapport. Indirectly observe the breathing cycle of another person and try to match it as closely as possible. This can be difficult because of the natural difference in most people's breathing cycles, but if you are able to maintain the mirror you will be rewarded with a powerful connection. This works wonderfully with babies when you are trying to put them to sleep. The feeling of rapport is very comforting and peaceful, and will settle them down quickly.

External Energy Work

Internal energy work is a great start and unquestionably leads to many benefits in a person's life. Increasing your energy flow breaks down barriers within yourself that keeps you separate from The Quantum. Moving your energy externally offers advanced benefits which allows you to interact 'magically' with your environment. This includes energetic projection and out-of-body experiences.

Moving Consciousness:

This most basic of exercises is very similar to the initial exercises you practiced when working with your chakras. The goal is to move your consciousness to other parts of your body. Select a spot on anywhere on your body and put all of your attention and focus there. Concentrate on this spot until you feel it tingling or buzzing — until you recognize some noticeable change in sensation at that spot. Play with it. Like you did with the chakras, you can spin it, bounce it, breathe in and out through it. Select another random spot on your body and see how fast you can recreate the sensation.

Moving Subtle Energy:

Let's go out-of-body now. This is an exercise that when repeated often enough will result in a full OBE, but can be considered a minor OBE all by itself. You can do this exercise regardless of where you are or what you are doing. Simply imagine that you reach out with your arm *without moving your physical arm* and touch something near you. Feel the 'movement' of your arm in your shoulder and its weight in your chest and lats.

Experience the texture and temperature of whatever it is you are touching. For example, as I am writing this I am reaching out to a flowering geranium on a table halfway across the room. I can feel the thickness of the dark green leaves and their slightly hairy texture. I'm using past experience of touching similar leaves to viscerally experience the feeling. Practice this exercise as often as you can and in as many different ways as you can.

Walking Around:

This exercise is even more likely to lead to an OBE. Before going to sleep, I will viscerally experience pushing myself out of bed, standing up and taking a random walk around my house and property. I allow myself to experience these walks through my senses as if I were actually physically taking the walk. I always finish these "walk abouts" by returning to my bed and laying back down to give the sojourn a sense of closure. There is no danger of losing your soul or anything like that. If you do not return to your body — for instance, if you fall asleep while you are walking around — your energy will return of its own accord.

Repeating this and the previous exercise often enough will result in an actual OBE as your body and energy gets into the habit of moving external to your body.

Energy End State

Uninhibited Energy Flow is the foundation of The Visceral Experience. Everyone has an innate natural energy that flows through them. At its very lowest level this energy provides life, but to move up the evolutionary ladder, you must dis-inhibit and grow your energy flow. This is done through internal and external energy work and by removing the blockages that are discovered during that process. This process can take a long time and can bring up very difficult issues from childhood that need to be addressed or at the very least accepted before progress can be made. Raising your energy is a series of steps consisting of large jumps in energy followed by a plateau where new blockages are discovered. Once those issues are addressed the next level can be gained.

Once you have established a basic ability for manipulating your internal and external energy you will be ready to start taking conscious advantage of it by focusing on, and creating powerful intentions and advanced visualizations.

Advanced Visualization

I think, therefore I am. ~Renee Descartes

You may ask yourself, "How is The Visceral Experience different from the visualization methods you have already read about and mastered?"

Just as the combustion engine replaced the horse, the cow and the ox (useful though they were for their time), the technology of The Visceral Experience replaces, or updates, the concept of visualization. Those beasts of burden were useful and got the job done. They were able to pack and pull heavy loads for long distances in extreme conditions. But they didn't go anywhere fast and sometimes folks might have wondered if they were moving at all. That is my experience with older methods of visualization.

There have been many useful books written about visualization which have helped thousands, if not millions, of people better achieve their goals and improve their lives. *Creative Visualization* by Shakti Gawain was perhaps the first and is probably the most well known of this genre. Learning and practicing the visualization techniques she describes in her book is a good first step, but is pretty much hit or miss. Regardless, along with affirmations and setting your intent, it is good practice anyway.

Building on this, the movie and book *The Secret* by Rhonda Byrne arrived to much acclaim and success. Millions of copies of the books were sold and millions of people have watched the movie. Oprah did a show about the concept and yet all that was really said was that there is this thing called the "Law of Attraction" that will give you everything you want in life. Absent from the book, the movie, and the interviews is a *concrete* method for accessing this law. It was a feel-good book with a lot of hype, but it really didn't reveal any secrets. It certainly doesn't lay out concrete methods or strategies for utilizing this law; only generic, feel good, but generally useless things like, "think nice things".

Incidentally, the term "Law of Attraction" was first coined and defined by William W. Atkinson in his 1906 book Thought Vibrations or the Law of Attraction in the Thought World.

Yet, you might ask, if the techniques written about in these books worked, why is everyone not using them to make their lives better? Why are there still skeptics? Why is there still so much wrong with the world?

Unfortunately, much of the effectiveness of these techniques has likely been coincidental. Through an undisciplined practice of visualization, many have touched on the reality behind the facade and have thus achieved a modicum of success. Yet the real technology remains hidden and the process is not easily repeatable.

The problem is that neither of these books ironically reveal the real secret. Some books might come close to or even hint at the deeper truth, but none give the reader a clear and concise guide to reaching the proper level of focus; a level of focus that I call "The Visceral Experience". The Visceral Experience gathers a combination of techniques from numerous fields of study into one all-encompassing tool that is magnitudes of order more powerful than the individual techniques alone.

To put it another way: the visualization methods that these books describe is a two-dimensional technology in a three-dimensional world. The Visceral Experience adds the other dimension and opens the door into The Universal Consciousness. Manifestation? Healing? Astral travel? Relationships? Prosperity? Whatever your goal, it is much more easily

Daniel D. Barber

achievable once you have learned the core concepts of The Visceral Experience. The Visceral Experience is a learn-able and repeatable technology that allows anyone to take their interaction with reality to a whole new level.

Neuro-Linguistic Programming (NLP)

I introduced NLP earlier when discussing its uses in terms of energy work and establishing rapport. The primary application of NLP, however, has been in the field of psychotherapy. It shows great promise as a method for lessening the impact, if not the outright removal, of traumas from therapy patients. Therapeutically speaking, making a traumatic event less immediate and less intense via a visualization overlay, will reduce and hopefully eliminate the psychological response. NLP methods are successful at doing this because they are based on an improved understanding of how the human brain interprets, responds to, and maintains memories. The simple essence of that understanding — and the practical part that applies to visualization — is that the more intense and immediate the visualization, the more intense and immediate the experience.

Sensory Sub-modalities

"Sensory Sub-modalities" is a big term for something very simple. Each of our five senses are sensitive to a full spectrum of stimuli ranging from weak to strong, comfortable to uncomfortable, familiar to strange, etc., and all degrees in between. These are called sub-modalities in NLP and are very

Daniel D. Barber

important to The Visceral Experience. Below is a table of
example sensory sub-modalities.

Sense	Sub-modalities			
Visual (sight)	Harsh	Bright	Gray	Blurred
Audio (hearing)	Soothing	Cacophonous	Loud	Whisper
Kinesthetic (feeling)	Hot	Uncomfortabl e	Happy	Angry
Olfactory (smell)	Acrid	Sweet	Savory	Rotting
Gustatory (taste)	Sweet	Bitter	Salty	Sharp

What is important about sub-modalities? They are another
building block in creating a successful visceral experience.
Visualizations are stronger when fleshed out with all of the senses
and even stronger when customized with unique sensory sub-
modalities.

Let's start with the textbook beginner visualization:
visualize yourself on a beach. Feel the sun on your skin, the wind
in your hair, and perhaps some sand in your bathing suit. Smell
the salt in the air. Hear the waves as they break on the shore and
hear the seagulls as they cry to each other overhead. Enjoy the
sensation for a moment.

Okay. That's the basic version and the script is generally fine, but it is missing something: you must *truly* experience the different sensations to the point where you can feel it in your gut. Let your body and mind react the way it would if you were really at the beach. Use the different sensory sub-modalities to make it stronger. Do you feel the wind moving the hair on your head or arms? Does the intensity of the sun on your skin vary with the wind? Do you smell fish along with the salt in the air? Is the sound of the ocean soft or harsh, comforting or not? Does the sound recede with the waves?

Feeling it in your gut versus enjoying a pleasant feeling is the difference between an advanced visualization and your standard, run-of-the-mill visualization — and the difference between being successful in your energy work and spinning your wheels.

Now that we have an understanding of sensory sub-modalities, let's talk about viewpoint in visualizations, or as NLP terms them, 'perceptual positions'.

Perceptual Positions

Perceptual positions is a visualization model used in NLP to help people in therapy associate or disassociate from events. There are numerous perceptual positions, but in The Visceral

Experience only the first three are the most important. I like to think of them in terms of the 'first person', 'second person' and 'third person' voicings used by writers to establish point of view though the correlation is not exact. To disassociate from a traumatic event, the therapist would talk the client through a visualization process that starts out in first person (fully associated and completely immersed in the traumatic event), progresses through the second person (semi-associated), and ends at the third person point of view (fully disassociated).

Let's take an example visualization about improving your tennis game. Looking out of your own eyes in the first person point of view, you would visualize yourself holding the tennis racket and looking across the net at your opponent. You can feel the sweaty grip of the handle and the weight of the racket in your hands. You can feel the breeze on your face and smell the rubberized surface of the court. You are fully associated when you experience the game during your visualization in exactly the same way you experienced it when you were there.

In this example the second person perceptual position would be if you were watching yourself play tennis from the viewpoint of the umpire. You would be able to see your entire body and how 'you' move and react. This position has removed those parts of the visualization that are of immediate impact to the client and therefore makes it less *real*. This is a more objective viewpoint for visualizing and seems to be how the majority of people, in the tradition of Creative Visualization, visualize.

The third person perceptual position is yet another step removed from the main actor. In this position you would simply be the audience way up in the stands watching the umpire watch the main actor. From here the main actor is smaller and less clear, the colors are indistinct, and the sounds are muted. This position is useful from a therapeutic standpoint but is exactly the opposite direction from where we want to go.

When you are doing visualizations be certain to do them from the first person point of view. This is many times more difficult to achieve and sustain, but also many times more effective.

For the following exercises it would be useful to pick a minor traumatic event from your life to work with so that no harm will be done if something should go wrong. An inconsequential incident of embarrassment from your youth would be a good place to start.

First Person:

First, let's experience that embarrassing event again in the first person. Look out of your eyes as you make your way to the event. Feel the temperature and humidity of the location, smell the smells, re-experience the people and your internal state (fear, anxiety, stress, or lack thereof). Put yourself completely back in that time and event and re-experience it as if you were there. Notice your physical reaction to this re-visualization. Are you sweating now? Is your heartbeat elevated? Have you tensed your jaw muscles in reaction? This is the perceptual position one must be in to successfully use The Visceral Experience.

Second Person:

Now, let's back off a bit. Give yourself some time to come down from the last exercise and then let's start over. This time experience the event as if you were simply an observer on the sidelines. You will simply watch the events unfold as if you don't know the actors and cannot feel the location. You are completely objective and the event evokes no emotional response in you. Instead, concern yourself with simply observing as if you were taking notes for a newspaper article. This is the perceptual position most people find themselves in when using visualization techniques. This can be great for relaxation and meditation, but is not powerful enough for manifestation.

Third Person:

This position is the therapeutic pot of gold, but anathema to The Visceral Experience. In this position you remove yourself even further from the prime actor and the immediateness of the event. In this scenario you observe the second person actor watching the prime actor. The prime actor and the event in question are much smaller and nearly indistinct without any of the sub-modalities discussed above. Observe the events like a reporter would, but this time the focus of your observation is the second person — the other reporter at the event. Colors are gray, smells are non-existent, etc. Repeat the event in your mind from start to finish from this viewpoint and observe your physical reaction, or lack thereof, as you progress through the time-line. To remove the trauma of this event from your psyche, repeat this third person point of view over and over until you have absolutely no physical or mental reaction.

Visualization End State

Visualization entails much more than just mental images. The most powerful visualizations incorporate all of the senses with associated intense sub-modalities. The end state of a

Daniel D. Barber

successful visualization is a physical reaction in yourself. You should be able to experience the visualization in some physical manner whether it is by breaking out in a sweat, by sliding into a relaxed state or by some other somatic reaction. Once you start physically experiencing your visualizations you have reached an adequate level of advanced visualization.

Powerful Intention

Nothing is more active than thought, for it travels over the universe, and nothing is stronger than necessity for all must submit to it. ~Thales

Aleister Crowley, the famous English occultist, once famously said, "`Do what thou wilt` shalt be the whole of the law." While completely misunderstood by the masses, something he probably didn't mind all that much, he was exactly spot on. What he was really saying is that *your reality reflects your true will*. It does. The real question is, *what* is your true will?

Determine Your Current True Will

Just as astronomers can glean amazing amounts of information about unknown and unseen worlds by studying the shadows and gravitational wobbles of other celestial bodies, we can glean some interesting information about our true will by studying our current reality. Take notes on where you are right now in your life, what you like and what you don't like about your current circumstances. Do bad things keep happening to you? Do you find recurring accidents or sickness for you personally, or for family, friends or acquaintances? Do you keep repeating the same mistakes when choosing a love interest? Are you never able to get ahead financially? Take notice of these repeating cycles and consider what thought patterns or actions of yours are creating or contributing to these patterns.

Make a list of "goals" that would describe your current reality. These goals reflect your current *true* will. These are the goals that you have focused on enough, unconsciously or not, to turn them into intentions. These are the intentions that have become your reality.

An example list of bad goals:

- I like intense feelings of love that don't last
- I will never find someone to love me
- I am a mediocre employee
- I will be stuck in this job forever
- I will never make enough to buy nice things
- I can't save money
- life isn't fun

This list is the place to start when coming up with a re-worked list of goals. It might be as simple as modifying one word in one of your current goals to change your entire reality.

Set Goals

Okay, like all of those other self-help methodologies, I too include a section on keeping a list of goals. It can be important to write out those goals in a place where you can revisit them from time to time, daily if necessary. I've put my list on my private website in an easily editable wiki that I keep for my various projects. Here is my list:

- Get Married. Check!
- Have Children. Check!
- Increase to infinity patience. Still working on this one, but making progress.
- Explore my ability completely. Still working on this one, and making progress.
- Write a song. Check!
- Finish screenplay. Still working on this one.
- Write book *The Visceral Experience. Check!*
- Work on / make a movie. *It's True You Know… Check!. Naked Fear. Check!*

Some of these goals I've accomplished and some I'm still working on. I like to keep them all on my list so I can revisit my successes. This helps me associate a positive feeling with my list will then transfer to my other as of yet unaccomplished goals. This is the first tool in creating a powerful intention.

Affirmations

Our inner voice has a powerful influence on our lives. It can be the source of our greatest inspiration or our greatest detractor. The difficulty for many of us lies in keeping that internal voice positive and encouraging. We all fail from time to time and when we do it takes no conscious effort on our part for that voice to become negative or ridiculing. It does that automatically with no work whatsoever. Many times it repeats negatives that we've heard in the past from people whom we've loved or respected. Subconsciously we have taken their words and internalized them. It is the lucky few amongst us who have internalized only the positive words from people they love.

Unlike your list of goals above it is important to remove or modify affirmations once they have been achieved. If you fail to do so you run the risk of implying to The Quantum that you are not satisfied with the results. And that might undo the results you've already achieved. This is especially true if your affirmations automatically become your intention (see below).

Constructing Affirmations

Affirmations can be a powerful tool for setting your internal dialogue and, thereby, for setting your intent. Effective for a variety of purposes, one constructive use is to reset your current internal dialogue to something positive and uplifting. Another would be to focus on what you wish to manifest in your life.

Regardless of your goals, affirmations are an important tool for creating powerful intentions. The rules are fairly straightforward.

Short and Simple

In my experience, keeping affirmations short and simple with a single, focused goal is more effective than long, convoluted affirmations which hit all the bases. Short and simple phrases are easier to remember, easier to viscerally experience and more effective in general. In fact I sometimes break my goals into smaller pieces and construct multiple affirmations for each smaller piece.

Present Tense

Affirmations should always be phrased in the present tense using the word "Now", if time-frame is referenced at all.

This is setting the stage for The Visceral Experience and forcing the current reality to conform to your expected reality.

Meaningful To You

Many books about affirmations reference deities, higher powers and other myths that may have great meaning and impact for the author, but may not mean anything to you or I. A general rule: if it doesn't mean squat to you, it's not going to do squat for you. Construct your affirmations so that they are meaningful to you. If you believe that Odin is still the God-King and is the creator of the universe then add a supplication to Odin into your affirmations. If it is meaningful to you then that importance and the weight of that importance will be translated into The Quantum along with your request. If you add a supplication to something that means nothing to you then that sense of 'meaning nothing' will be carried on into your supplication and will be ignored.

Easily Visualized

You know you have a good affirmation when it is easily accompanied by an advanced visualization. As you repeat your affirmation, viscerally experience it with all of your senses. Doing so will cement the affirmation and the associated feelings in your subconscious. That's powerful stuff, right there. Now whenever you repeat your affirmations the feelings will return, even if you are not accompanying them with visualizations.

Examples:

As an exercise, let's say I want to construct affirmations that will help me build a powerful intention for getting a new pair of skis. I might use the following affirmations.

1. I love my new pair of skis
2. I love the bright colors and the design
3. I love the smooth finish
4. I love the new bindings
5. My new skis look wonderful with my ski outfit
6. My new skis really cut into the snow when I turn
7. I am flying by everyone else
8. My control is really smooth and effortless

Each of these affirmations can also be easily incorporated into visualizations.

- Imagine the wonderful feeling you have when looking at, touching and examining the new skis. (1,2,3,4)
- Imagine the compliments you receive, or the approving looks you get, when wearing or holding the skis. (5)

- Imagine the feeling you get when actually going down the hill; the g-force you pull when making sharp turns, the wind biting your skin, etc. (6,7,8)

Intention End State

Setting your intent is at once the easiest and by far the most difficult of all disciplines we will discuss in this book. It is easy in that it is a natural process which all of us do sub-consciously every day. It requires discipline though to do consciously.

Setting a goal of having more money, happiness or love is a no-brainer for most of us. Who couldn't use more of those things? After you have made a list of goals the challenge is to turn those goals into *intentions*. What's the difference, you ask? The difference is whether those goals are realized or not and depends upon the magnitude of focus you sink into the goal. If, like most self-improvement methods I've tried, you make a list and then forget about it, then the goals remain goals and remain unfulfilled. If, however, you focus your attention on that goal every waking moment over days, weeks, months and even years, then you have created a powerful intention that will be realized.

When I set out to have an out-of-body experience, I spent day and night reading everything I could about the process and practicing every method I could find that made sense to me. At the end of three weeks time, I had my first OBE and was able to continue experiencing OBEs while my focus lasted. My OBE phase lasted until I took a new job that dominated my attention and left me no time or energy for other pursuits. But, during those six months that I was actively working on OBE, I was able to gain a measure of control over the experiences and even direct them to some extent. Those OBEs still rate among the highlights of my overall experience with energy work. This is partially because of the intense, paradigm shifting effect these experiences had on my view of reality and partially because they happened so early in my efforts at energy work.

Daniel D. Barber

Putting It All Together

Except our own thoughts, there is nothing absolutely in our power. ~Rene Descartes

Every person is able, as a matter of course and without learning any additional skills, to practice the technology of The Visceral Experience. It is an inborn skill through which we create and experience our reality. Everyone does it every day and the reality you are experiencing right now is the result of the human race's cumulative visceral experience.

Learning and practicing the component skills allows us to take a more direct hand in changing the nature of the reality we create. The quicker we can relax, the easier we fall into our light trance, the more free-flowing our innate energy, the more visceral our visualizations and the more powerful our intentions, the more impact we will have on our reality.

When it comes right down to it, The Visceral Experience is a gut feeling — that's it. The trick is learning how to create that gut feeling such that it will have a discernible effect on your reality.

In Practice

Daniel D. Barber

Energetic Projection

A chief event of life is the day in which we have encountered a mind that startled us. ~Ralph Waldo Emerson

Energetic projection is a term I've coined for a psychic ability that I've not been able to find documented or labeled elsewhere. In short, it is the ability to effect another person's somatic (physical) and emotional being solely through an ability of the mind. It is an extension of the concept of rapport (which I consider to be a weak energetic projection in that the connection can be broken by either party at any moment), however, it is magnitudes of order more powerful and can be initiated and maintained by a single party.

I am, to my knowledge, the first person to label and describe energetic projection as an ability separate and unique from other psi abilities. In that I am still learning how to work with and use this ability, the full scope of its effects are still undefined. Currently I know that I can induce emotions and feelings such as fear, familiarity, friendship and even sexual excitement in another person. These emotions, as has been well documented in numerous studies, have a secondary physical effect of increasing heart rate, core temperature and even skin conductivity (galvanic skin response). I also use energetic projection as the basis for my technique of energy healing which I'll discuss in the next section.

The ability to utilize energetic projection results directly from mastering the basics of The Visceral Experience. This capability extends beyond working with other humans to interacting with plants, animals and even inert electronics and technology — though I've yet to delve deeply into those aspects of this ability.

Methods

The method here is really the same as I mentioned above when discussing external energy work. You will simply viscerally experience interacting with an external subject without physically moving. With a person, for example, one could viscerally experience giving that person a warm, loving hug by feeling that person's skin and hair beneath your hands, their warmth on your chest, their breath on your neck or shoulders and their scent in your nostrils. Recreate with this person a great hug that you've had in the past from someone else. The way The Quantum works is that some of the feelings and images you get will probably be supplied by the other person.

Daniel D. Barber

Experiences

In the experiences I describe in the following pages my attempts at energetic projection caused significant, consistent and repeatable reactions from the subjects; reactions that were out of the norm for the circumstances; reactions which convinced me that my energetic projection was the cause. Once I had an idea that something out of the ordinary was happening I approached the whole thing as a mystery that begged to be explored. During the process of exploration I have taken some wrong turns and ended up at some dead ends. However, it is not necessarily the results that matter, but the journey. The following instances are only a couple of examples from a vast array of experiences that I've had.

Beyond NLP (Way Beyond)

One of my first experiences with energetic projection was on an hour-long airplane flight with the passenger seated next to me. I had been reading about Neuro-Linguistic Programming (NLP) and creating rapport by mirroring the other person's actions. Being that we were seated next to each other, it would have been really awkward to mirror actions, so instead I chose to mirror her breathing. This is a fairly difficult thing to do without seeming 'creepy' unless your direct observation of the other person is expected. We were, however, sharing an armrest and our arms were comfortably touching. Through the combination of feeling her breath through her arm movements and observing her peripherally, I was able to match her breath for the majority of the flight. This is not as easy as it sounds. Her breathing cycle was shorter than mine so I would intermittently have to take a deep breath in order not to pass out. But, all in all, I was as successful as one could could expect.

During the flight, I had absolutely no indication that any effect had been achieved. As I matched her breathing, she didn't pull away or distance herself or act repulsed in any other way. Of course, if she had, I would probably have been very embarrassed and stopped mirroring right away. But she didn't and I continued until we separated to retrieve our baggage from the overheads. At this point, I thought it had been a nice exercise and a comfortable flight; nothing more, nothing less. But when she scooted out into the aisle (I was already out and standing), she turned and looked up at me with such a deep and meaningful gaze that I had to look away. I found I couldn't meet her gaze and instead acted like nothing at all had happened — that I hadn't been doing anything. She turned and that was the last I saw of her.

Daniel D. Barber

This was my first experience with energetic projection (though I didn't realize it until later) and it occurred a full two or three years before I tried anything else. This really was just me practicing NLP methods and I did not realize what a huge room there was behind this door. I opened the door again sometime in 2005.

Best Friends

This is a method that I have used many times with great success. When I walk up to the counter at any retail store or restaurant I viscerally experience myself as the absolute best friend of the person waiting behind the counter. The exact scenario I imagine depends greatly on the person and the initial feel I get from them, and sometimes I get scenarios that I feel are precipitated more by them than by me. A scenario that I have used many times is to imagine myself at a barbeque with the person, arms around each other's shoulders, beers in hands and both of us laughing uproariously at some joke. The reception I get when the person turns their attention to me is one of great welcoming and, many times, the person really wants to interact with me even if, to this point, they had only been perfunctory with those who preceded me. If this had only happened once I might have written it off as coincidence, but this type of reception

126

happens consistently when I use this method. Another method I have used is to viscerally experience hugging the person which results in a similar reception.

Intimidation

Energetically projecting violence is not something I like to do. I won't even do it anymore in situations like the one I describe below. This is because I realize now that we are all one and the same. We are all a part of the same energy and consciousness. Any damage I do to that person, I do to myself. Talk about self-defeating. If, however, circumstance puts me in a position where I need to act for my own or my family's safety, I will act however I must. This is just one tool in the toolbox. At the time I attempted the following, energetic projection was still new to me and I wasn't even sure if it was real or just an illusion of mind.

Waiting for my order at a burger joint, a young tattooed, wife-beater-wearing gangster came to wait next to me. He didn't try to intimidate me, but his whole demeanor was one of intimidation. His dress, his swagger, his backwards cap and his general attitude; danger and intimidation poured off him. Using an opportunity to test my new process I energetically projected myself violently grabbing his throat and choking him. His image already in mind, I did not need to look at him to do this and his reaction was not subtle. Within moments and after a couple of glances my way he had put as much space between us as was available in the small area. Except for my efforts, there was no other reason for him to distance himself.

Energetic Projection and Reality

The ability to project your energy and have a physical effect on another person demonstrates that we are all but facets of a single entity, The Universal Consciousness. That it is possible to reach across time and space and have a demonstrable effect on another person's physical and emotional being is absolutely mind boggling — unless viewed through the lens that we are all One. Once you accept concept of The Universal Consciousness, not only does this type of interaction become explainable, it also becomes the rule. You will notice this energetic interaction in everything you do and with everyone you interact. It becomes inescapable.

Energy Healing

Healing is a matter of time, but it is sometimes also a matter of opportunity. – Hippocrates

After my revelatory experiences with energetic projection, I wanted to see where else I could go with my explorations. Healing with energy seemed a natural progression, and I was lucky enough to be friends with a cranio-sacral therapist who was willing to trade sessions. I learned some of the basics of cranio-sacral therapy, which is very much about exchanging energy with the client, and was able to incorporate that into how I worked with energy. Still my process very much included using energetic projection to effect change and healing both on myself and on others.

The effects of energy healing are many times ambiguous as the results of a healing session may not become apparent for days or even weeks afterward, and even then the results may not always be attributed to the energy work. In the mind of a skeptic, positive results are *never* the result of any energy work the client may have had. Confirmation bias is a funny thing; it works both ways. There have been, however, studies that have proven the positive and sometimes miraculous results of energy work. The book, *Energy Cure* by William F. Bengston chronicles his attempts to study energy healing on mice that had been artificially given a very deadly strain of a breast cancer gene. Will studies like this ever satisfy the skeptics or the dogmatic? Not likely, but then whether the doubters believe is not important to the results of healing. Bengston even showed in his studies that belief by the client was not a necessary factor. Energy healing exists and is effective regardless of belief or lack thereof.

Methods

My energy healing method is a natural progression from my earlier work with energetic projection. Similar to energetic projection, I actively push energy into and through the recipient. When I first started my work with healing, I read books and tried methods that others had said were successful for them, but I felt like I was trying to understand someone's illegible handwriting. When I disregarded their methods and started following my own path, I began to see results in both myself and with others.

Pushing Energy

Pushing Energy

With my hands on the person I will feel the energy flow through my body into the other person as I relax into a slight (light?) trance. The energy will come up into my heart chakra, through my shoulders, down my arms and out through my palms. When I begin a session I will go through this movement very slowly in my mind feeling the energy move very specifically through each body part and even into the other person. Once I have established the flow, I will relax my attention a bit and let the flow move on its own as much as possible. I will accompany this flow with an intention of healing.

The Slinky

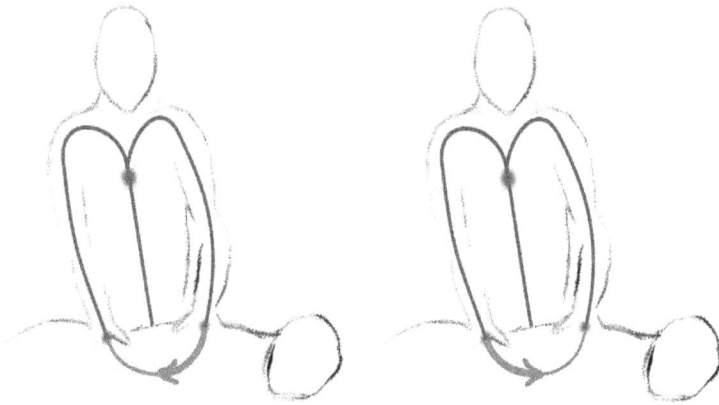

The Slinky

After I have established a connection by pushing energy, I will bounce energy back and forth between my hands. There is a curious push-pull dynamic going on when doing this. The effect feels to me the same as when I used to bounce a Slinky, the spring shaped wire toy popular in the 70s, back and forth between my hands when I was a kid. There is a curious push-pull dynamic going on when doing this. This seems to help me establish an energetic connection between my hands and I'll use this to springboard to the next step, Cycling Energy.

Cycling Energy

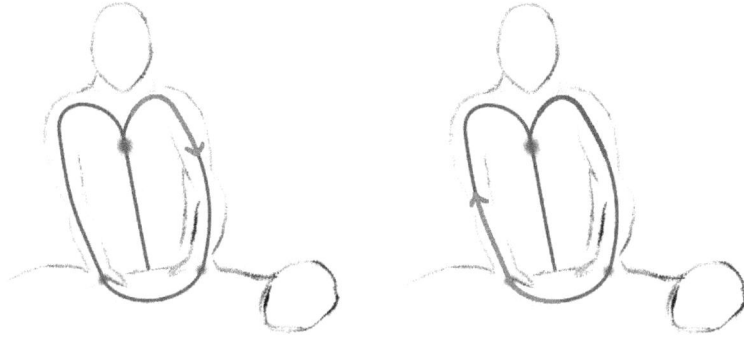

Cycling Energy

Again with my hands on the person, I will begin by pushing energy from my heart into my left shoulder, down my left arm, through the palm of my left hand, through the person, into the palm of my right hand, up my right arm, through my right shoulder, across the back of my neck and back down into my left shoulder repeating the cycle. With practice this becomes easier to maintain without specific attention to holding the flow. This method I got from the book *The Energy Cure* by William Bengston. It differs only in that I do not accompany the cycle with dynamic visualizations, which I think is something he does to help him achieve the proper trance state. I don't feel this is necessary if you are able to achieve that state on your own. It certainly has not been necessary my work.

Filling The Container

Filling the Container

This exercise I will do only after establishing a strong energetic connection through previous methods. I imagine that a stream of energy is flowing from me to the client in a steady stream, like milk into a glass, slowly filling the person with light and energy. I continue this until I have filled the client to the top with light.

Reaching In

Some of the most successful healings I have accomplished have been when I have viscerally experienced reaching into the body and gently massaging the affected body part, whether it be heart, skin, gums, or whatever. Without any knowledge of anatomy, besides what I have been able to pick up from living forty odd years, I am able to imagine the body part and its function, and effect change by viscerally experiencing it in its healthy state.

Experiences

Palpitations

A problem I had been experiencing intermittently since beginning my energy practice has been an irregular or palpitating heartbeat. Not too long after starting trades with the cranio-sacral therapist, the palpitations grew worse and were more consistently present. They occurred on a daily basis, in fact. I assumed this uptick was the consequence of having an increased energy capacity and fewer energy blockages within my own body. Using the quiet listening I learned from cranio-sacral methods I viscerally experienced myself placing my hands inside my chest and gently massaging my heart muscle. I pulled off scabs from old wounds and gently caressed my heart until it was smooth and healthy. The effect was immediate; the strength, duration and frequency of the palpitations significantly lessened. After this first effort, the palpitations dropped to about once a week and were not nearly so concerning to me. I repeated this same process numerous times over the next two weeks until the palpitations ceased completely.

Soothing Baby

My youngest daughter, Elena, started teething when she was three months old and is now, at two and a half years, working on her last tooth. She's had it much more difficult than my oldest daughter, Anja, who at least had some breaks between the worst of the pain. When I get a chance to put Elena to bed I would perform some gentle healing on her. The timing with this is tricky. If I push or cycle energy into her and she is not quite asleep, I run the risk of energizing and keeping her awake a bit longer. If I time it right, the energy will quickly take her down to a deep slumber. Often the twitching of beginning dreams will quickly accompany my energy work.

Stopping Hiccups

One night, as I was putting her to sleep, Elena was battling a rough case of hiccups. They were constant enough that she was not able to close her eyes for more than a moment before having to hiccup. Putting myself into a light trance I viscerally experienced reaching into her chest and gently massaging her diaphragm. Again, not being a physician, I have never actually seen a diaphragm. But that does not seem to matter much. What I imagined was similar to a camera aperture made of muscle. Using my thumbs I gently massaged the muscles and viscerally experienced them relaxing under my touch. Elena's hiccups stopped immediately.

I've since repeated this success when Elena was across the room. It was very early in the morning and I was just waking up. My wife was taking an awake and hiccuping Elena downstairs into the living room. With a quick visceral experience, I repeated my previous method and her hiccups stopped immediately. I fell back asleep.

Energy Healing and Reality

What does this ability *not* say about reality? I was able to instantly stop my daughter's hiccups from across the room simply by using a visceral experience. You might think this was my energy interacting with hers, but that places a false barrier where there is none. In actuality I changed The Universal Consciousness. We are all one energy and one consciousness.

Out-of-Body Experiences (OBE)

Be sure that it is not you that is mortal, but only your body. For that man whom your outward form reveals is not yourself; the spirit is the true self, not that physical figure which can be pointed out by your finger. ~Cicero

After experiencing lucid dreams and learning of OBEs, I looked everywhere for more information. I was consumed with the idea of going out of body. Luckily, the internet, while relatively new to widespread use, had some informational resources on both OBEs and lucid dreaming. I read these with interest. I also found William Buhlman's book, *Adventures Beyond The Body* to be an excellent guide and I highly recommend it to those who wish to attempt an OBE. Going out of body may not be a prerequisite for a visceral experience, but it will certainly strengthen your belief, ability and control.

Being out of body is a great way to communicate directly with your subconscious or your guides (however you prefer to view it), to get answers and to set goals. Overcoming the fear that one experiences when first out of body is the major obstacle followed closely by the difficulty in remembering the goals and ideas that one set while awake.

Methods

All the methods for OBE incorporate a couple of shared attributes. The first is that you have to be absolutely wide awake during the attempt, otherwise it is likely that you will simply fall asleep. The second is that you have to be absolutely relaxed and in a light trance. The third is that you have to imagine yourself actually getting up out of your body. There are a couple of variations on the last, including floating out or rolling out. For myself, I found that when I was sufficiently relaxed, I would sometimes spontaneously float out without too much effort. The difficult part at that point is in maintaining a calm so that you do not tense and immediately pop back into body. *Adventures Beyond the Body* has a full discussion of methods and techniques to get out of body, as well as advanced techniques to use once out.

Sinking Mantra

This exercise could also be considered a meditation and, in combination with other factors, is actually a strong exercise for attaining OBE. Lying on your back, repeat the mantra "relax" with each exhale as you feel yourself sinking into the bed. Your breath should be slow and comfortable; not strained in any way. If discomfort arises, acknowledge it and discard it without effort, returning quickly to your relaxed mantra. After a while you may begin to feel like your body has become a shell and notice subtle energy effects, such as a disassociation from your extremities to the point you can't really tell where they are or how they are situated.

Push Up

Once you get to that point of disassociation, viscerally experience, without physically moving, doing a push up out of your body. When you do this successfully, you'll notice an increase in vibration along your body and maybe even a noticeable sound commonly described as a loud buzzing or ripping. These sensations will increase until you actually achieve separation.

Roll Out

Some people find this method more comfortable, although I've used both successfully and without problem. This time, when you feel you are disassociated enough, simply viscerally experience yourself rolling out of your body. You will notice the same energetic sensations and sounds.

Experiences

Buzzing and Ripping

The intensity and volume of the sound, which could only be described as a ripping or buzzing noise, took me by surprise the first time I went OBE. I was not asleep, nor had I fallen asleep, when this occurred. I had been practicing meditation and relaxation lying supine on top of my bed in the middle of the day. My mind was alert and I was quite aware, as a curious tingling feeling crawled up my legs and into my torso just before the event. And yet, I was still surprised when I achieved separation. I was only out for a moment before losing the mental discipline necessary to stay out, and popped back in to my body.

To this day, I think of that ripping sound as the sound of my subtle energy body separating for the first time from my physical body, ripping from its physical moorings. It was only after this event that I began to experience the other psychic-related events of which I speak about in this book.

Going Through the Ceiling

One of my first experiences had me separating from my body, with the by now familiar sound of ripping, and floating up. With a conscious choice, I decided to go out into the night air, and did so by going straight up through my ceiling. I could feel the energy of the physical ceiling commingle with my own energy, and traverse my entire body from head to toe as I passed through.

This was a revelation to me; first, that I could move my subtle energy body through physical objects, and second, the feeling of the ceiling's energy sliding through me.

Being Observed

I don't remember much about this trip, except that I went out and became aware of myself standing waist deep in dark water. Or rather, it was night and everything was dark. As I looked around, I became aware of another entity watching me. He was also in the water and fairly close to me, but the water came up to just below his nose and he was wearing a full face/head mask in several shades of blue, such that even his eyes were covered. I was not scared of him in any way, but rather comforted by his presence. I don't remember what happened after this encounter. It was a fairly short experience and I think I may have popped back into my body shortly thereafter. This was different from my 'Eye of Infinity' experience, in that I still felt like I was completely in control — I was not overawed by this observer, like I was by the other entity.

Daniel D. Barber

The Park on the Hill

This was the proverbial 'Heaven' experience. I went OBE and, after using a couple of techniques to increase my vibration learned from William Buhlman's *Adventures Beyond the Body*, I found myself under a bright blue sky at the foot of a large hill crowned by a mighty tree and carpeted with beautiful green grass. There were many people on the hill engaged in various, clearly joyful activities. I was not there long, nor did I interact with any of the beings, but I returned to my body with an extraordinarily peaceful feeling.

Do I think that I actually visited Heaven? No, not in the traditional sense. I believe I experienced the same archetypal location that others have visited and have labeled as heaven. Not believing in organized religion, I won't put a label on it myself. Was it a peaceful and happy feeling? Yes. But, by no means do I believe it is our final destination. It is simply another level in the astral, perhaps the last before moving into the Universal Layer and experiences like the 'Eye of Infinity'.

The Ghost at the End of the Bed

I became aware that I was out of body when I was standing next to my bed, and my physical body was still there under the covers. The room was dark and the atmosphere oppressive. A nearly overwhelming fear grew in me as I looked around and saw that sitting at the end of my bed was an entity, wrapped completely from head to toe in my favorite comforter. I stood paralyzed for a moment while I wrestled with the fear and considered my options. Recognizing the fear for what it was — unfounded and unreasonable — and steeling myself, I grabbed the comforter and yanked. There was nothing there.

The OBE and Reality

If the boundaries between us truly are illusory (and they are), then one should be able to move their consciousness outside of their body (one can). Extending energy beyond the bounds of the physical body is the next step in a natural progression of energy work, moving from internal work to external with more power and control.

Going out of body does not mean that one is invisibly walking around and exploring our own world; rather it is that your consciousness, now unmoored from the physical, is exploring the energetic dimensions of reality. When out of body, one is able to jump to higher frequencies of vibration — the lower frequencies being closest to our waking reality, the higher frequencies might best be associated with higher beings.

The lower frequencies of an OBE mirror waking reality, but are not exact duplicates. If you enter an OBE with fear in your heart, the lower frequencies can be very dark and oppressive, and the fear you experience there will be debilitating. To be able to get to the higher frequencies, one must be able to overcome the fear one experiences in the lower.

I am convinced that it is in these lower frequencies where most 'hauntings' occur. I've had several experiences when I went out of body inadvertently and didn't know it, perhaps transitioning from a nightmare. Not knowing that I was OBE and being in this dark, oppressive lower frequency, fear hit me like a ton of bricks, nearly overwhelming in its intensity. And usually, there is an entity there (a construct of our own mind, perhaps representative of specific fears we hold inside). By simply acknowledging my fear and confronting the entity, I have been able to overcome these base fears, and hopefully, putting whatever issues they represented in my subconscious to rest.

If the lower frequencies are closer to waking reality, then the higher frequencies are something else entirely. These are the levels where people might encounter aliens or heaven, both constructs of the mind experienced while the mind is attached to our subtle energy body.

Manifestation

Everything you can imagine is real. ~Pablo Picasso

Our current reality, the one we are all experiencing right now, is a manifestation of our own and our ancestor's collective powerful intent, as unflattering as the idea of that may be. The downside of evolving an increased intelligence as humans have over the millenia, is an inflated ego and all the negatives that can be attributed to that. This is the result of not understanding the power and beauty that we embodied as part of The Universal Consciousness, a power and beauty that one can witness being played out every day in the animal kingdom. Humans are now distinct from, though still a part of, The Universal Consciousness. As such, we have to work harder re-establish that connection. We have to overcome our fears and our ego. We have to overcome old traumas and self-delusions. And, most of all, and possibly the most difficult to achieve, we have to be aware that we have to do these things!

Increased ability to manifest one's 'true will' is a natural consequence of increased skill in the methods of The Visceral Experience. I have used it successfully numerous times to bring about changes in my reality and circumstance. I count my wife and children, my current job and location as examples of my ability, my wife's ability, or a combination thereof, to create a visceral experience.

Successful manifestation of a conscious intent may be the crowning achievement of one who is working on their psychic abilities. It is not the easiest thing to accomplish and requires discipline, dedication and massive focus. Even when one has the intense focus, one must also have established at least a partial foundation of unrestricted energy flow, or the energy required for manifestation is diverted by our ego into other, sometimes negative, avenues.

Methods

The method for successful manifestation is simply the method of The Visceral Experience, with an emphasis on the second pillar, powerful intention. Elsewhere I talk about powerful intention and how to create one, but for completeness, I'll include the basics here as well. Assuming one has opened up their energy flow and has at least basic ability in visualization, one must set an intention which they wish to manifest.

Goals

Whether it be love, money, a specific accomplishment, a new skill, or something else, write it down as a goal. Let's say, for example, you want a new car (so do I). Add it to your list of goals — be specific as to make, model, color, features, etc.

Affirmations

Write out and add an affirmation to your daily ritual. Remember, it should be stated in the positive, should be stated in the present, should be short, easily visualized, and it should be meaningful to you. For a new car, I might use the following affirmations:

- I love my new car.
- I love the smell of the leather interior when I slide into the driver's seat.
- My new car handles amazingly.

Visualizations

Each affirmation, if possible, should be accompanied by an advanced visualization. For a new car, I might use the following visualizations:

- I love my new car. (Visualize it in your driveway; feel the smooth finish as you slide your hand over the driver's door, see the light shine off the roof in the color you desire).

- I love the smell of the leather interior when I slide into the driver's seat. (Feel yourself open the door and slide into the leather seat. Smell the leather).

- My new car handles amazingly. (Feel the steering wheel in your hands and the smooth acceleration as you take a turn. Experience the Gs as the car hugs the road).

Create a Powerful Intention

- Refer to your list of goals numerous times a day, paying specific attention to the goal of attaining a new car.

- Repeat your affirmations to yourself every chance you get, with the accompanying advanced visualizations.

- Wherever and whenever you can, read books, articles, reviews and whatever you can about that car.

- Wherever and whenever you can, watch videos and listen to reviews of that car.

- Learn as much about that car as you can, always keeping in mind the features you want.

- If you wake up in the middle of night, fantasize about that car.

- If you have down time during the day, daydream about that car.

- Every chance you get, wherever you are, focus your thoughts on that car.
- Do the above until you have manifested your desire.

Experiences

It is not possible to definitively prove the success of my attempts at manifestation, but the one that provides the clearest example was just before moving to Santa Fe and into my current job. The back story is long, perhaps too long for the point I'm trying to make, but I'll give just a bit.

My wife, my new baby and I were living completely off-grid in Taos, New Mexico. It was a wonderful experience living in a passive-solar earthship[2] utilizing solar electricity and capturing all of the water necessary for our needs from our roof. We were so off-grid that we even had an outhouse that, with the door swung open, provided a beautiful thirty mile view of the high desert, from north to south. I've watched herds of elk stampeding across the valley plain while doing my business. I've also found a rattlesnake curled up beneath the toilet seat — thankfully before sitting down. Still, the outhouse was definitely one of my favorite aspects of the whole experience. Unfortunately, jobs were difficult to find out there and with a new

---

2   http://earthship.com

baby, I was feeling the need to start bringing in a steady income. We were also so remote that emergency services were either forty minutes away on a good day, or on a bad day, available only by helicopter.

When Anja was three months old, my mom called with an opportunity at a local manufacturing company in their small hometown in Kansas. Yes, Kansas. Not having any other options at the time, we took them up on their offer, packed up and moved out to small town Kansas.

It was a difficult transition for my wife and I. With a new three-month-old that we were still learning how to care for, we were sleep deprived and continuously tired. We were living with my parents in a town new to my wife and one which I had lived in before, but had never liked. I was working for the only manufacturing company in town, which was run by people with small-town mindsets, or I should just say small minds. These were the types of people who judged you not by your actions or character, but by which town you grew up in. People from towns more than thirty miles away were considered foreigners and were not welcomed. My wife grew increasingly unhappy from incidents like being openly stared at in public as if she were some misshapen monster, or attending parties where no-one would

152

engage with her in conversation. All in all, it was a very unpleasant seven months that we were there.

> As with any situation, there were exceptions to the unpleasantness. There are several families that live in that little town that are true gold; kind, open, happy and warm, and we have missed their company since moving away.

After six months of working in that claustrophobic little plant, and with no job and no prospects, I quit. But Ann and I did have plans and intentions. After about three months, we had started setting our intention to move on. We had picked Santa Fe, New Mexico as our desired location and I had set my mind on finding a job in my semi-specialized field within IT. We talked about moving on daily, I started to put my resume out there, and Ann had started to look through real estate listings. It was with this daily focus that we set a powerful intention. Within weeks of quitting, and on the same exact day, I received two job offers. I took the job that was in Santa Fe. It wasn't until later that I realized how few jobs there are in Santa Fe for someone with my skill set. Had this particular job not been open, the likelihood of us getting there would have been practically nil.

Manifestation and Reality

The ability to manifest one's desires shows that reality is a two-way street; it is not just happening to us, it's interactive. We can cause reality to conform to our desires and to provide us with what we need. Reality can be as pleasant or as unpleasant as we wish; we simply have to set a powerful intention.

The more enlightened of us can manipulate reality on multiple fronts of their lives — money, fame, health, etc. But for those of us still struggling to achieve enlightenment, one must be careful not to damage other parts of our lives. For instance, having all the money in the world will not help if your health declines rapidly. Or, it may not be worth having if you have no one to share it with.

Challenges

Or Opportunities?

The belief that there is only one truth and that oneself is in possession of it seems to me the root of all the evil that is in the world ~Max Born

As you make progress with The Visceral Experience method, you will encounter many different types of challenges that must be overcome in order to proceed to the next level of psychic mastery or enlightenment. I say challenges, but they might better be considered opportunities; for each challenge, if accepted and overcome, brings with it an increase in the frequency at which your energy body vibrates. In other words, you advance towards enlightenment. The changes after each success may be imperceptible to you at the time, but taken together with past successes, the change becomes obvious.

Those Around You

The people you surround yourself with, and their biases, preconceptions, misconceptions and fears, have an affect on you. Their negative energy, as they saying goes, "will bring you down". In order to grow in your ability, you may have to break from the dogma of your particular group — which will likely have an effect on your standing within the group. This is difficult for many to do, especially if your new beliefs become common knowledge. You may become the object of ridicule or scorn, as dogmatic people often react with anger to those who challenge or disregard their beliefs.

Skeptics, Atheists, Realists

Of course, The Quantum being The Quantum, if one does not accept the concept of a Universal Consciousness as the above named group does not, then The Quantum complies with your will and you get what you expect — a solidly physical and non-spiritual existence. The energetic action between people becomes a simple mystery, ignored in one's own life and disputed or disbelieved when others bring evidence to light. These are our skeptics, atheists and realists. Quite honestly, I cannot imagine living a life so cut off from others.

At least in a general sense, though, I consider myself to be a part of the realist group. I guess I just differ with most of this group on what exactly constitutes reality. And that is the problem with most of these types; their skepticism, realism or atheism is really just a reaction to Christianity, or whatever religion is dominant in their family tradition. Like a whiplash, they have reacted so severely that they are not open to other possibilities or interpretations of reality. And funny enough, even with their withdrawal from religion, their mindset is still absolutely grounded in the traditional thinking of their forefathers. For example, they see spirituality as being a choice between some kind of theism and nothing; black and white, binary, all or nothing. But reality is anything but that.

Be aware that you will not convince these folks of your version of reality, nor will they accept any anecdotes of your experiences as proof of anything except that you are probably going a bit looney. The most that you will accomplish by interacting with them is to cause yourself doubts, for psychic experiences are ephemeral, like a dream, in nature — at least until you have integrated these capabilities to the extent that they are a part of you.

The Oblivious

Most members of organized religions are simply members of their particular dogma because of family or community tradition. Their religion, like their genes, has been passed down from generation to generation, given less thought than what will be served for dinner on Sunday night. These are the oblivious masses, with few exceptions.

The exceptions are the folks who have become aware that there is something besides the solid physicality presented to their senses. They are aware that there is something more to reality than the skeptics would admit. And yet, because of their religious tradition, they attribute that 'something more' to this or that god. Unfortunately, they give their power away to a non-existent god, and in the process deprive themselves of the only means for discovering the truth.

The Indoctrinated

The indoctrinated are even worse than the oblivious because they have crossed the line into fanaticism. They lead the way in indoctrinating the next mass of the oblivious. They are the fundamentalists, the born-again and the fanatics, who disregard reason, common sense and logic in favor of the words of their holy book of choice. These are the dangerous people who will attack you for not believing as they do. Stay away from them.

The Spiritual

Whether they be New Agers, yoga masters, mediums or you-name-it, these folks are on a more correct path, and a path that could eventually lead them to a clearer understanding of reality. They understand that organized religion is the wrong path. They realize (or hope) that they have power, as an individual or as a group, to interact with reality. The secret that they have discovered is that reason, intelligence, a spirit of discovery, and an open mind is more likely to lead one to the truth than a two-thousand-year-old book written by meagerly educated men of the time. Of course, as with every group, there are dogmatists for whom this involvement is more about power and money than it is about truth. That is simply human nature. Regardless, minus the dogmatists, these are the people with whom you want to surround yourself as you dig into The Visceral Experience.

The challenge here is to discard the chaff and find the thread of truth. This can be difficult with all of the competing theories and frameworks. I was able to get to this point myself by disregarding those theories encumbered by esoteric terms, secrets, dogma, ceremony and hierarchy. That is not to say that there is no value in some of those theories, just that the information is available elsewhere, without having to first spend time as a 'novice' or 'adept', or first level whatever.

The Angry, Judgmental, Divisive, and Jealous

These folks are negativity incarnate and will suck your energy from you. Remove these negative influences from your life if you can, and surround yourself with positive, harmonious and happy people. You'll notice a positive change in your own energy when you do this, and a positive change in your own spiritual progress.

The Disbelievers

I was working with another energy healer who suffered from scoliosis, a curvature of the spine. It was becoming more pronounced with age and severe enough that she was seeing a chiropractor about it. I was very excited to work on her given that I had never had the opportunity to work on a skeletal condition before. During our first session, I worked intensively with my mind on straightening her spine, viscerally experiencing exerting pressure on the spine to straighten it, imagining using clamps to force it into place, passing intention through my energy that her spine was straight and pretty much everything else I could think of that might have some effect.

I remember, in particular, imagining that I gripped her spine from her lumbar vertebrae to her cervical vertebrae and forcefully pulled to straighten it. Where I ran my hands I had the perception that her spine turned red. I didn't purposely imagine that color, it just happened as I did the exercise. During the same session, she had asked that I also work on her gall bladder, which I did almost as an afterthought. I imagined, as I did for my heart palpitations, that I massaged the gall bladder and that it was smooth and healthy under my fingers.

The next time I spoke with her, she said that she felt nearly ill the afternoon following our session, but she attributed that to hormones and her cycle. I was too naive and new with healing that I did not rebut her, though anyone who practices healing knows that sometimes after a particularly intense healing your body may find itself in turmoil as it processes its new reality. She had even discussed this balancing process before in some of her own writings.

Two or three weeks later, she told me how her chiropractor had noted significant improvement in her spine. She primarily attributed this improvement to the work done by her doctor, but told me that my work "had helped a little". She also reported that she hadn't had any further issues with her gall bladder, a change which she attributed to an improved emotional state on her part.

I tell you all this because it is illustrative of the mindsets that people hold that are difficult, if not impossible, to break. This idea of reality being physical and mechanical is so entrenched in the human condition that it is even difficult for other energy healers to accept. If they can attribute positive change to a source that is more comfortable for their pre-conceived world view, then they will. William Bengston recalls similar interactions in his book, *The Energy Cure* — people would come for healing, would notice improvement, but would never return for further work. It can be very frustrating.

Spiritual Growth

Life is a series of natural and spontaneous changes. Don't resist them - that only creates sorrow. Let reality be reality. Let things flow naturally forward in whatever way they like. ~Lao Tzu

Traumas

As humans, we're all loaded with tons of neuroses and baggage, whether from our childhood, previous incarnations, or just stuff that we are supposed to work out on behalf of The Universal Consciousness. These are the obstacles we must address, overcome or accept in order to move on to the next level; in order to increase our own vibratory rate, in this incarnation or the next.

Our past traumas will rise up and confront us as we proceed towards mastery of The Visceral Experience. This is a good thing and should be seen as much as an opportunity as a challenge. Accepting and overcoming our past traumas allows us to shed the associated negativity which keeps us grounded at lower frequencies. As we increase our vibratory rate by overcoming old traumas, the next layer of traumas will rise up to block our way, challenging us to accept and overcome these too.

Hopefully the issues we are confronted with will decrease both in width and breadth, as we become more and more adept at The Visceral Experience.

Life Rules by Yehuda Berg is a book written for teens about the Kabbalah. Even as an adult I found it to be well written, clear and very convincing in regard to the benefits of changing yourself from being a reactionary to being an observer when confronted with situations that would normally be inflammatory to us.

The Essence of Reality by Thomas Nehrer reaches similar conclusions regarding overcoming past traumas and spiritual growth. His book is an excellent read on the nature of reality.

Old traumas are like a straitjacket. Overcoming a trauma is like loosening the belts a notch, which allows us to grow and stretch a bit until we are encumbered by the next restraint. I have found that moving from reaction and attachment to observation and detachment when reliving traumas has allowed me to move forward. I am by no means divested of all of my issues (I have a lifetime or more of them to work through), but I am making progress and feel I have found a method that works for me. While I can share the methods that work for me, I can by no means make the assurance that the same methods will work for you.

That is an answer that only you can find. The books above are excellent places to start.

Fear

Mostly due to my experiences with OBE I associate fear with the lower frequencies of reality and the lower or more base instincts of humanity. Fear leads to, and can be manipulated into, anger and violence. It plays a role in our level of stress and our stress response, which in turn has an impact upon our health. Fear is the fodder from which "the abyss" is constructed.

Alternatively, I associate the lack of fear with the higher frequencies of reality. The lack of fear, or the feelings of security and stability, is an essential ingredient for the realization of happiness and joy. I believe fear is the primary challenge of our physical existence. Fear is the driving force behind much of the bad we experience in life: anger, violence, bigotry and divisiveness. Fear is a contributing factor in greed and the desire for power. As adults our lives are ruled by the fears that we succumbed to as children, which was visited upon us by the fear, in one of its many forms, experienced by our parents, friends, family and others.

The freedom we feel when we surmount our fears and open ourselves to love and acceptance is something amazing to experience.

Natural Tendencies

Growth, by definition, comes at the expense of the old. The old habits, the old mindsets, the old tendencies; all must be discarded to allow the new to take hold. This process can be an enormous struggle. Your natural tendencies are habits that have collected, like barnacles, over your entire lifetime and can be very difficult to "scrape" off.

My most challenging tendency is impatience, a trait that I have struggled against my entire life. It remains a challenge for me because I put myself in a mental space wherein I lose my perspective and get so caught up in events that I am unable to appreciate the insignificance of whatever problem is affecting me. Although I still struggle with the tendency, I have improved a thousandfold times since I've been married, and a thousand more times since I have had children.

Everyone has issues which interfere with their mental processes, ability to relax, or some other aspect of spiritual growth which must be overcome. This is the nature of life and our daily struggle as human beings. The best we can do is recognize our challenges and strive to overcome them.

Experience Your World.

Daniel D. Barber

The Elegance of The Visceral Experience

Simplicity is the ultimate sophistication. ~Leonardo da Vinci

The beauty, simplicity and power of The Visceral Experience lies in the fact that it is something we do every moment, every instant, every nanosecond of our lives. Just like The Quantum is omnipresent, so is our interaction with it. Because we are *of* it. By learning the technology of The Visceral Experience we are simply learning to do better what we already subconsciously know how to do.

Workshops, Conferences and Speaking

I am available for workshops, conferences and speaking engagements in amenable forums. Challenging, thought provoking and fun, my talks can last between one and two hours depending upon audience interaction.

Self-Healing Facilitation

I am also quite happy to work with individuals for the purpose of facilitating self-healing.

Recommended Resources

The following books have all influenced my thinking one way or another. These books contain thought-provoking discussion and mind-expanding exercises. I hope that by reading through them you will gain insights that will complement, correct or even expand upon the ideas I've presented here in *The Visceral Experience*.

- *Instant Rapport* by Michael Brooks
- *Adventures Beyond the Body* by William Buhlman
- *Energy Work* by Robert Bruce
- *Energy Cure* by William F. Bengston
- *The Essence Of Reality* by Thomas D. Nehrer
- *Life Rules* by Yehuda Berg

About The Author

Dan Barber has been exploring the mental, visceral and spiritual world of reality for the last twenty years. Dan's interests are eclectic, ranging from trying to bake the perfect loaf of bread at home to playing guitar to raising his children such that they may have fewer traumas to work through in their own lifetimes. Since writing the original version of this book, Dan has become a certified Hypnotherapist, Master Neuro-Linguistic Programming (NLP) Practitioner and Cognitive Behavioral Therapist (CBT). He lives in Northern California with his wife and daughters. This is his first book on the subject of spiritual growth compiled from years of notes and experiments.

Connect with Dan

Follow Dan at http://facebook.com/wisethirdeye.

Appendix A

Theoretical Physics

There is no unique picture of reality. ~Stephen Hawking

Before we dive fully in the technology of The Visceral Experience, it is important to understand the reality that we currently live in, its nature and how it supports the conclusions I've reached.

> **If theoretical physics is not your bag, then skip to the end of this chapter to the sections entitled Experiential Reality and Reality Summarized.**
> There, I've posted my conclusions about the nature of reality. It is not necessary to agree with all of my conclusions to be able to use the skills discussed in this book, but they may help you reach your potential faster. If you do decide to skip the discussion in this chapter, then spend some time with the summary points which follow and try to give yourself a basic understanding and acceptance of each — even if you do not necessarily agree with them.

The State of Scientific Research

Science, as a method of inquiry, has been validated many times throughout the centuries. The evidence of its value is everywhere in today's world: from the technology I am using to write this book to the technology used to send men to the moon. Science as an institution, however, has become bankrupt and rotten on the inside, and is quickly losing the trust of the public. The scientific community as a whole has failed in its primary duty of objective inquiry, and the resultant distrust has been well earned.

Chief amongst the reasons for this loss of trust is the death-grip that funding has on the process. Scientific inquiry today is limited to the direction given by corporations and governments because those are the organizations that provide the money for the research — corporations in pursuit of the all-mighty dollar and governments in pursuit of power and control. Even worse is that only the research that results in positive outcomes for those respective agendas is likely to be published. According to Ben Goldacre in his TED[3] talk, upwards of fifty percent of medical research goes unpublished for that very reason.

Another failure of modern science is its inability to re-examine initial assumptions. This is found throughout the field Initial assumptions and models are clung to even though ample evidence to the contrary has been brought forth and accepted by the larger community. The anatomy of an atom is a great example of this. The electron was 'discovered' in 1897 by J.J. Thompson. Thompson didn't actually see the particle, but intuited its existence based upon his observations of a cathode ray. His

3   http://www.ted.com/talks/ben_goldacre_battling_bad_science.html

intuitive leap is now considered unquestionable fact. This, in and of itself, is not a big problem. Answers are often arrived at through intuitive leaps. The problem begins when behaviors that do not fit with the hypotheses are explained away in increasingly unlikely ways.

When an atom gives off energy, it is hypothesized that the electrons in orbit around the nucleus drop from a higher orbit into a lower orbit. The bit that doesn't make sense is that the electron does not cross the intervening space between orbits. First, the electron is in this orbit, then whammo! It is instantly in the smaller orbit. It would be one thing if this were observed behavior, but it is not. It is behavior that is hypothesized in order to make the electron fit in with the *assumption* that an electron exists, i.e., if the particle called the electron exists, then it must act in this manner.

Additionally, electrons are still considered to be monopole particles (i.e., lacking both a positive and negative pole) which has never been observed anywhere else in nature. Again, if this conclusion was the result of observation, that would be one thing; instead, however, it is the product of deduction based upon assumption.

Now consider that quantum physics posits that subatomic particles don't exist at all.

In a classic case of mistaking the map for reality, the model used to simplify and teach atomic physics is now considered to be how reality actually works. Electrons, neutrons and protons are useful to explain the characteristics of an atom, insofar as they are not misleading, but they rest in a purely Newtonian understanding of reality, e.g., this ball with such and such mass hits that ball with such and such mass, which results in the second ball going somewhere. We have known since the 1930s that Newtonian physics does not apply at the subatomic level. When are we going to change and update the textbooks?

These are the contortions that make up modern physics.

Particle physics has never been re-examined through the lens of our new understanding; the revelations and lessons of quantum physics have never been applied cleanly to our understanding of the atom. Physicists are still looking for the higgs-boson, because they are still convinced that there is no way that mass could be the result of anything but the property of a particle. They view mass as the result of adding an object which

Daniel D. Barber

already has mass to the atom, not as a mutable attribute of the atom itself.

The third failure rests in the pride and ego of the scientists themselves. Pride is perhaps one of humanity's biggest failings and it is no less so in the field of science. Those men and women who have worked their entire life in a field of study, and whose reputations are cemented in their research, do not succumb easily when some young upstart scientist proposes a theory that challenges previous conclusions. Estimates are that it takes two generations for challenging truths to be recognized and accepted, which is approximately how long it takes for the old-guard to ride off into the sunset of retirement or mortality. Two decades to overcome the bias of the current generation; that's not long in the overall scheme of things, but perhaps too long in respect to the lifespan of a human.

Science is no longer a wild west of exploration, though we surely know less than one percent of one percent of all there is know. Science has become mired in its own success, much like a too-successful company when the MBA's take over from the innovators. Regulation, fiscal concerns and red-tape have replaced curiosity, adventure and the sense of exploration that was common to the thinkers of eighteenth century.

Gone are the days when a wealthy patron would allow an intrepid explorer to follow their whimsy in search of truth for truth's sake.

What We Know

Regardless of the current state of science, let's take a look at what we actually know, courtesy of unimpeded scientific investigation.

Subatomic Particles

Subatomic particles do not exist. Period. There is no such thing as a particle that exists as a self-limited, discrete object. Electrons, neutrons, protons are theoretical constructs we have used to this point to understand the attributes and predict the behavior of atoms.

Instead, there are vortexes of energy which are not self-contained and are not discrete from the rest of existence which can be, and have been, mistaken for particles. These vortexes of energy display attributes such as mass, charge, velocity, and direction of movement, and yet, because they are not separate from their constituent energy, cannot be treated or analyzed in a Newtonian fashion. They don't interact with each other in the

manner of billiard balls. They interact with each other in a
quantum manner, which is far more difficult to understand.

Atoms

We know atoms exist, because atoms make up molecules
and molecules are the building blocks of everything we see. For
example, if we take two atoms of hydrogen and one atom of
oxygen and allow them to bond, we then have a molecule of
water, or H2O. We know enough about how molecules and atoms
work to break this bond in numerous ways and to separate the
hydrogen from the oxygen. This allows us to make use of the
individual atoms in other ways.

Unfortunately there is a massive amount that we don't
know about atoms, and especially its constituent parts, if there are
any. Current subatomic theory suggests that atoms consist of
electrons, protons, neutrons, etc. which in turn are made of more
and more exotic particles such as muons, gluons, etc. Of course,
in order to get this anatomy to align with observed behavior,
particle physicists have to hypothesize additional dimensions,
particles and symmetries. They also have to ignore other
established scientific theories (including the full theory of
gravitation) because those theories would throw off their
calculations. In other words, modern particle physicists are

frolicking in a playground of their own making which has very little to do with reality.

Zero-Point Field

There is no such thing as a true vacuum. Even in the emptiest container in the emptiest part of outer space, and even at a temperature of absolute zero, there remains a very subtle energy called the zero-point field. In this field, these vortexes of energy (normally, and mistakenly, referred to as particles) pop into and out of existence of their own accord. This field is the potential from which everything else is generated; the stem cells, if you will, of reality, and exists not only in outer space, but everywhere — around you, inside you, within the earth and at the farthest reaches of space; this field permeates existence. Or maybe it is existence. I will refer to the zero-point field alternatively as "The Universal Consciousness" and "The Quantum" throughout this book, depending on context.

Albert Einstein

With the equation e=mc2 (energy equals mass multiplied by the square of the speed of light), Einstein calculated that mass is the same as energy and energy the same as mass, the only variable being the speed or frequency at which the atoms vibrate. This equation, part of Einstein's Theory of Special Relativity, has

Daniel D. Barber

been experimentally proven many times and in many ways. Mass and energy are two faces of the same coin; two attributes of the same primal object.

This theory jibes perfectly and beautifully with Walter Russell's hypothesis that all atoms are photons. Read on…

As an interesting side note to this, but not necessarily related to The Visceral Experience, Einstein continued, "Furthermore, the equation e=mc²… showed that very small amounts of mass may be converted into a very large amount of energy and vice versa."

Not only are we energy, but each of us is a **MASSIVE** amount of energy. All of the energy in a nuclear bomb is released by fusing two hydrogen atoms and forming a helium atom. The difference in energy is released explosively when this happens. We are, each of us, billions and billions and billions of hydrogen atoms, approximately 4,550,000,000,000,000,000,000,000,000 (4.55 billion billion billion) hydrogen atoms according to best estimates[4], not to mention the other types of atoms contained within us which could also be split/fused. The amount of energy contained within each of us is absolutely staggering.

---

4   http://science.howstuffworks.com/atoms-in-person.htm

Walter Russell

The Atom

Walter Russell, a genius polymath who died in 1963, hypothesized that atoms of all types are simply photons with different spins — for example, the difference between an atom of hydrogen and an atom of uranium is simply the vector and speed of the gyroscopic motion of the photon. Using his model of atoms Russell was able to lay out a periodic table of elements in his book *The Universal One*, 1926, that accurately predicted several elements which were unknown at the time including plutonium, deuterium and tritium. It even successfully predicted elements that were not forecast by the standard model periodic table. His model of the atom provides a simplified framework for understanding the building blocks of matter and has yet to be seriously challenged.

Russell's table incorporates the golden ratio, harmonics and octaves in its organization. The golden ratio, as you might know, is found everywhere in nature — from the design displayed by the seeds on a sunflower to the spiral arms of distant galaxies. Harmonics and octaves are integral to the art of music which is, itself, integral to nature. Truth, I find, is often reflected in simplicity and synchronicity. The image which follows, from

Daniel D. Barber

Russell's book, *The Universal One,* displays the simplicity, beauty and symmetry of his version of the periodic table. This table is constructed using his idea that photon spin is the prime differentiator between atoms.

His model also displays a synchronicity with what we know about atoms from quantum physics: namely that there is no such thing as a subatomic particle. Inconsistencies which exist within the current model such as how an electron 'particle' will suddenly and instantaneously jump orbits as the atom gives off energy are no longer necessary when an atom is viewed instead as a three dimensional sphere of spinning energy. It is the spinning energetic motion of this vortex that gives the atom its mass and electrical charge and which identifies it as an atom of a particular type, e.g., hydrogen, helium or plutonium.

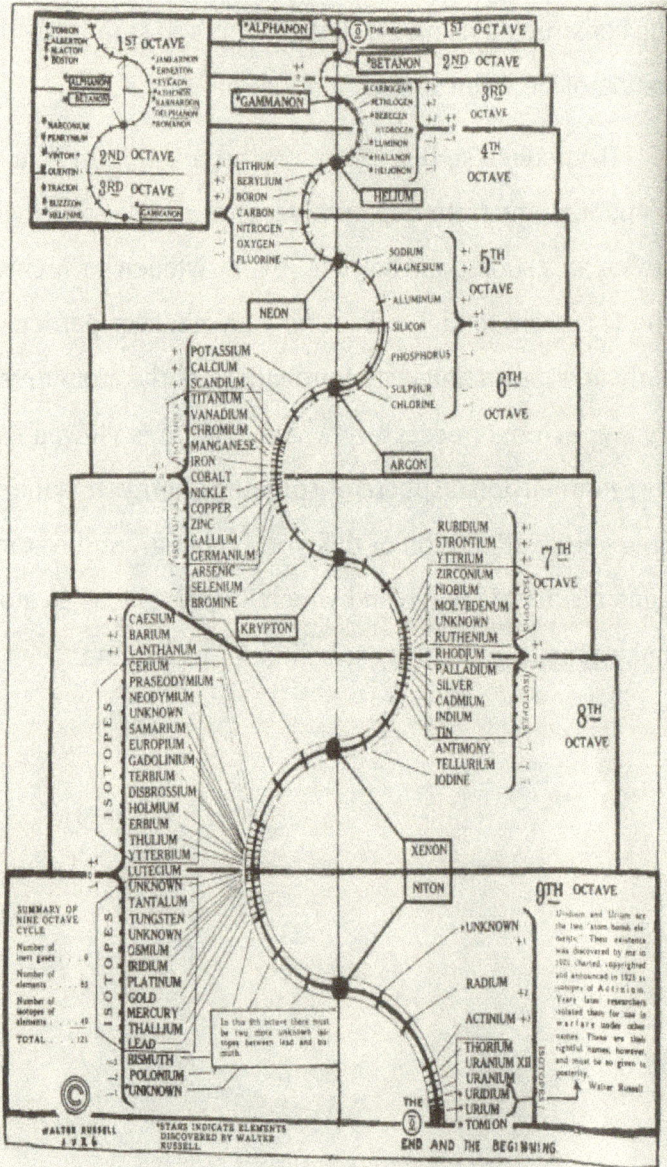

Walter Russell's Periodic Table of Elements

Daniel D. Barber

Zero-Point Field

If a particle doesn't give an atom its mass, then what does? To answer this we must take into account the zero-point field.

It is the motion of photons against the vector and frequency of this field that gives the photon its attributes of mass and charge. The closer the photon is to congruency with the field, the closer it is to zero charge and zero mass. In other words, the closer it is to being just a photon. The more the photon differentiates itself from the field — the more *friction* between the photon and the field — the higher up the periodic table the element will fall and the more exotic the element will be.

Russell's model for understanding the atom is intuitive, simple, displays symmetry, is harmonious with nature and has been experimentally validated. It can only be due the previously listed failures of science that his model has not been further accepted, tested and studied.

Quantum Physics

The Double Slit Experiment

This experiment was originally performed by Thomas Young in 1803 to prove that light propagated as a wave rather than a particle. In this he was successful but, at the same time, his results raised questions about the nature of light and reality that are still unanswered today. In the original experiment Young took a light beam from a single small hole in a window blind and split it into two to examine how the separate beams of light acted in conjunction with one another. The interference pattern (a property of waves) that resulted proved that light acted as a wave since particles do not interfere with each other.

With the replicable results of Young's experiment the particle theory of light propagation died out. However with modern equipment the story became a bit more complicated. When reducing the light to single photons fired like marbles one at a time at a board with two parallel slits the interference pattern was again produced, but the light that did show on the backing board consisted *entirely of particles*. This behavior, known as wave/particle duality, is crazy! Let's talk about the two experiments.

Daniel D. Barber

Experiments

First Experiment:

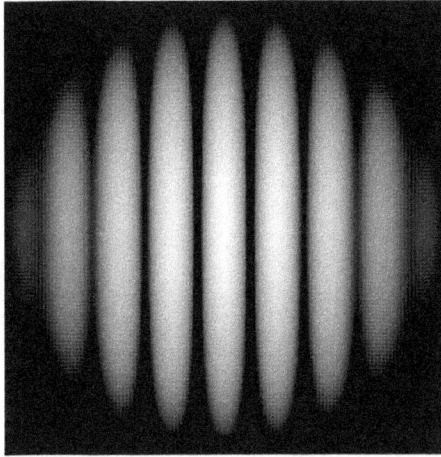

Double Slit Experiment – No Observation

In the first experiment (no observer), the photon is generated and shot out of the lab equipment. As soon as it has left the barrel (really another measuring device), the photon diffuses back into pure potential and rides the wave of the zero-point field at the 'speed of light'. After passing through the two slits and being broken into two separate streams, the photon interferes with itself in a wave-like manner, until it hits the backing board (the second measuring device). At this point, the photon collapses back into its particle form having been 'observed' by the backing board.

Second Experiment:

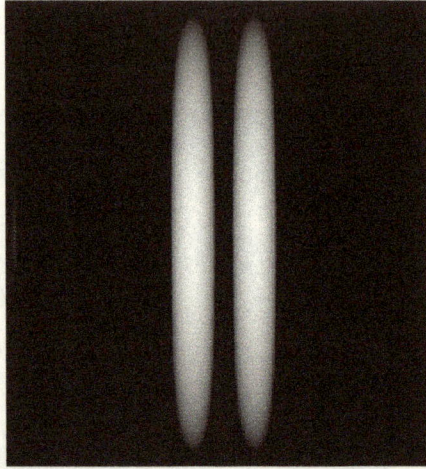

Double Slit Experiment -- With Observation

In the second experiment, another measuring device is introduced into the path after the slits to determine either the location or the vector of the photon. The experiment starts out the same. The photon is generated and shot out of the lab equipment. As soon as it has left the barrel (really another measuring device), the photon diffuses back into pure potential and rides the wave of the zero-point field at the 'speed of light'. Here is where things get wonky. The photon somehow knows, before passing through the two slits, that a measuring device is on the opposite side (It can only know this through some 'faster-than-light' mechanism, since the photon is traveling at the 'speed of light'). Knowing the location of the measuring device, the photon collapses into

Daniel D. Barber

particle form and picks one or the other of the slits to pass through, thereby negating the interference effect produced when passing through the slits as a wave.

Let's talk about that a bit. The photon acted one way when allowed to do its own thing without being observed, but when it was being measured, it acted a different way. What!? Are photons intelligent? Can they somehow know when they are being watched? Evidently, through some mechanism, they do know.

The mechanics behind this behavior are not well understood and has engendered numerous hypotheses to try to explain the results.

Interpretations
The Many Worlds Interpretation: From Wikipedia: "The many-worlds interpretation is an interpretation of quantum mechanics that asserts the objective reality of the universal wave-function and denies the actuality of wave-function collapse. Many-worlds implies that all possible alternative histories and futures are real, each representing an actual 'world' (or 'universe')." [5]

The Copenhagen Interpretation: "The Copenhagen interpretation is one of the earliest and most commonly taught

_____
5   http://en.wikipedia.org/wiki/Many-worlds_interpretation

190

interpretations of quantum mechanics. It holds that quantum mechanics does not yield a description of an objective reality but deals only with probabilities of observing, or measuring, various aspects of energy quanta, entities which fit neither the classical idea of particles nor the classical idea of waves. According to the interpretation, the act of measurement causes the set of probabilities to immediately and randomly assume only one of the possible values. This feature of the mathematics is known as wave-function collapse. The essential concepts of the interpretation were devised by Niels Bohr, Werner Heisenberg and others in the years 1924-1927." [6]

Of the two, The Copenhagen Interpretation has the most experimental proof behind it, makes the most sense to me and conforms most closely to my experience with altered realities and psychic experiences. The many worlds interpretation, where a new universe is spun off every time a choice is presented and a decision is made, is so far out there that it even makes me uncomfortable. Regardless, both interpretations are so close to sci-fi that they make most scientists itch in their shorts.

---

6 http://en.wikipedia.org/wiki/Copenhagen_interpretation

Daniel D. Barber

Explanations

To my mind, there are only two ways to explain this behavior.

The first way to look at it is that 'the speed of light' is actually the speed of photons riding on the wave that is the zero-point field — they have no innate speed themselves; it is the zero-point field that gives photons their speed, much like a cork in the ocean. The cork has no speed in and of itself, but is propelled along by the waves in the ocean. The frequency of that carrier wave therefore must be greater, and likely far greater, than the speed of light. If that is the case, it would be trivial for the photon to utilize some manner of communication with itself that is fast enough to traverse the zero-point wave in time to make a decision on how to act before reaching the slits.

The second way to look at it, and I believe the correct way, is that as the photon is created out of the zero-point field before being fired, and as the zero-point field, the standing wave of reality, is already aware of the measuring device, the photon is already aware as well. This hypotheses does not require faster-than-the-speed-of-light speed to explain this behavior, simply an understanding that all subatomic particles exist only as potential until we try to measure them in some manner. Regardless, neither of the above hypotheses changes the fact that the photons modify their behavior based on observation, and arguably, intent and expectation.

Consolidation of Three Hypotheses

The theory of special relativity teaches us that mass and energy are two attributes of the same object. Walter Russell posits that atoms of all types are simply photons, differentiated by vector and speed of spin, which, in turn, impart the attributes of charge and mass to the photon. The double slit experiment shows us that photons are created out of the zero-point field and are influenced by the intentions and expectations of observers.

The reality that these three, experimentally proven, vantage points describe is much different than what one normally thinks of when talking about reality. It is a difficult departure to make (impossible for some) and a significant shift of paradigm, to go from thinking of the world as solid and physical to thinking of it as energetic and ethereal. Even for those of us who have accepted this new paradigm, it can be a struggle to actually *experience* the world in that way.

In other words everything is made of energy, and more specifically photons, if Russell is correct. You, me, the chair you are sitting on, the table you eat at and the earth you walk on are

Daniel D. Barber

all comprised of energy. Mass is simply an attribute of those photons, as is charge. What's more, photons are influenced by thought. Everything (absolutely everything!) is influenced by thought!

www.ingramcontent.com/pod-product-compliance
Lightning Source LLC
LaVergne TN
LVHW011156080426
835508LV00007B/430